Common sense PARENTING®

SECOND EDITION

of Toddlers and Preschoolers

Common sense SECOND EDITION PARENTING®

of Toddlers and Preschoolers

BRIDGET A. BARNES, M.S.
STEVEN M. YORK, M.H.D.

Foreword by
THOMAS M. REIMERS, PH.D.

Boys Town, Nebraska

Common Sense Parenting® of Toddlers and Preschoolers
Published by The Boys Town Press
Father Flanagan's Boys' Home
Boys Town, NE 68010

Copyright © 2015 by Father Flanagan's Boys' Home
ISBN-13: 978-1-934490-71-6

Boys Town Press is the publishing division of Boys Town, a national organization serving children and families.

Publisher's Cataloging-in-Publication

Barnes, Bridget A.
Common sense parenting of toddlers and preschoolers / Bridget A. Barnes, M.S. and Steven M. York, M.H.D. -- 2nd edition. -- Boys Town, NE : Boys Town Press, [2015]

    p. cm.

    ISBN: 978-1-934490-71-6
    Includes index.
    Summary: For parents, disciplining young children should be more about teaching than punishment, and more positive than negative. This second edition of "Common Sense Parenting of Toddlers and Preschoolers" includes enhanced parent skills with updated parent steps and a clearer explanation about when and why to use them.--Publisher.

    1. Discipline of children--Handbooks, manuals, etc. 2. Toddlers--Discipline--Handbooks, manuals, etc. 3. Preschool children--Discipline--Handbooks, manuals, etc. 4. Child rearing--Handbooks, manuals, etc. 5. Parenting--Handbooks, manuals, etc. 6. Parent and child--Handbooks, manuals, etc. I. York, Steven M. II. Title.

HQ774.5 .B37 2015
649/.122--dc23   1502

10 9 8 7 6 5 4 3 2 1

Table of Contents

Acknowledgments

. . . .

We extend our sincere appreciation to the families that have shared their parenting joys and challenges with us throughout the years. We also want to thank our colleagues Laura Buddenberg, Kathy Kirby, Linda Schuchmann, and Erin Green for their feedback, support, and guidance on this newest edition of the *Common Sense Parenting of Toddlers and Preschoolers* book. And last, but certainly not least, we express our deep gratitude to Father Steven Boes, Dr. Daniel Daly, and Boys Town's leadership for their commitment to continuing Father Flanagan's dream.

BOYS TOWN NATIONAL HOTLINE®
1-800-448-3000
A crisis, resource and referral number for kids and parents

Foreword

BY THOMAS M. REIMERS, PH.D.

There is a quote by the English poet John Wilmot that goes something like this: *"Before I got married, I had six theories about bringing up children; now I have six children and no theories."*

Before their first child is born, all parents have their own theories and ideas about how they will bring up their son or daughter. They have a long list of expectations, dreams, and hopes for their child. They also have expectations for themselves for how they will parent and raise their child. Before children, parents will often make comments like, *"I will never allow my child to..."* or *"My child will always..."* or *"I will not make the same mistakes I've seen other parents make."* Then, their children are born and reality sets in. And that reality does not always match the expectations they have set.

I often have parents tell me things such as, *"I can't believe my child did that,"* or *"Oh my gosh! I sound just like my mother."* So while parents find there is much joy and excitement in raising a toddler, there also are a lot of challenges.

Raising children, of course, is an ever-changing work-in-progress. As a parent, your job is never done. This is never truer than when your child is a toddler or preschooler. In the toddler years, your child is rapidly changing in so many ways – physically, emotionally, and behaviorally. And just when you think you have things figured out, everything changes again.

The good news is that Boys Town understands what parents of toddlers are going through and we've developed an effective parenting approach that can guide you through your child's early years.

Boys Town's *Common Sense Parenting of Toddlers and Preschoolers* provides an outstanding set of building blocks that can help you become the most effective parent you can be. The authors have combined decades of their own experience with the knowledge and expertise Boys Town has acquired from nearly 100 years of working with children to help you learn how to communicate effectively with your toddler, and, more importantly, how to mold and shape his or her behavior in a positive, productive way. This is a book that will not only make you a more effective parent, but also will enhance and build your confidence. You'll find yourself returning to this book over and over and recommending it to your friends and family.

The toddler years are full of excitement, joy, and, at times, frustration. With apologies to the poet John Wilmot, my advice is to leave the theory-building to others and take advantage of the practical parenting strategies you'll find in *Common Sense Parenting of Toddlers and Preschoolers* to help you navigate and enjoy your child's toddler years. That time will go by faster than you can imagine. With Boys Town's proven approach to parenting, you can make the most of every day!

Dr. Reimers is the Director of Boys Town's Behavioral Health Clinic and the author of the Boys Town book, "Help! There's a Toddler in the House! Proven Strategies for Parents of 2- to 6-Year-Olds to Survive and Thrive through the Mischief, Mayhem, and Meltdowns."

Introduction

* *

"I love being a parent, but sometimes I'm too tired to enjoy it."

Have you ever found yourself saying or thinking something like this? Mixed emotions are something every parent feels now and then, particularly if your kids are toddlers or preschoolers. Being the parent of a young child is both exhilarating and exhausting. It is the most important responsibility you will ever have, and it can be filled with some of the richest and most satisfying experiences in your life – like watching your child walk for the first time or say *"Dada"* or *"Mama."*

But you also know that parenthood can be filled with all kinds of extremes – tackling your fifth load of laundry of the day, dealing with your child's eighth temper tantrum, or rocking a feverish little one in the middle of a long night.

1

Parenting involves lots of learning by doing. That means parents are faced with many situations they aren't prepared for. They may respond instinctively and afterwards wonder if they did the right thing. They may lack self-confidence in their parenting abilities. All parents need to keep in mind that sometimes things go well and sometimes they don't. That's just part of being a parent.

Like most parents, you will occasionally need some help and advice when you are having a tough time with your kids. All parents occasionally doubt their effectiveness. That's why we developed *Common Sense Parenting*®. It offers you some easy-to-learn skills that we know are effective and practical teaching methods that can help parents build happier homes. We have taught these methods to tens of thousands of parents in classes across the country for the past few decades with positive results.

Why do our teaching methods work so well? We emphasize two things: the *head* and the *heart*. The *head* means using a logical, practical method of teaching your children skills to help them learn to be self-disciplined. The *heart* is the unconditional love you have for your children that enables you to support them as they learn and grow. One without the other is imbalanced and ineffective. Put them both together and you have a powerful approach.

Our teaching techniques offer you a variety of parenting tools that have worked for families from all backgrounds. Whether you're an excited "rookie" with your first child or an exasperated parent or grandparent with a difficult child, this parenting approach can help you.

We all know there are no such creatures as perfect parents or perfect kids. We live in a sometimes messy, imperfect world and we're going to make mistakes, no matter how hard we try. It's also true that no parenting program alone can solve all of a family's problems. It would be foolish to make such a guarantee. Our lives are too complex to have exact answers for everything. However, the skills you learn in *Common Sense Parenting* – the logical techniques and foundations for discipline – give you a blueprint for creating your own unique parenting style. Research studies done on the skills we teach are very positive. Parents report that they feel more confident and effective in their roles as parents and that their children have fewer behavior problems.

> "If you see the handwriting on the wall, your 2-year-old probably found a pencil."

You are your children's first and most important teacher. No one should have a greater impact on your kids' lives than you. That means you have to bring to the task all the love, patience, and energy you can muster. Through all of this, you will find that parenting is the most exciting challenge you will ever face.

As you begin to teach your children, remember that it takes time for them to learn certain behaviors. Even though your children are young, they may already have learned some bad habits that may be firmly established. Changing these behaviors won't occur overnight. Your children may resist your teaching at first and things may even get worse before they get better.

> Many children, especially only children, create imaginary playmates. They usually show up between 2½ and 3 years of age.

Think about some of the long family car trips you've taken. You had to stop a lot. Maybe someone got carsick. Perhaps you took a wrong turn. Maybe the car needed repairs. You began to feel like you'd never get where you were going. At times, you may even have wanted to turn around and forget the whole thing.

Just like that family trip, parenting may not always be a perfect journey. But the trip is still worthwhile and you can reach your destination through patience, hard work, and perseverance.

Another thing to remember is that all of our skills rely on one crucial element of parenting. That element is spending time with your kids. You can teach them only if you're with them. It's as simple as that. You can enjoy the richness of family only if you spend time together. It's absolutely, positively a must. It is the glue that holds a family together.

Good luck on your trip! You're on an exciting path toward becoming a better parent. Make the most of all your parenting opportunities. Your love, the abilities you already have, and the skills you learn in *Common Sense Parenting* will make a positive difference in how you care for and discipline your children.

Teach them well.

1

As They Grow

Understanding Child Development

● ●

M any of us have had the experience of sitting around a dinner table at a gathering of family members or friends. Someone mentions, just in passing, that his or her little Johnny now can recite the entire alphabet or has mastered some other childhood milestone. It's tempting to wonder why your little one, who is just about Johnny's age, can't do what Johnny's doing.

Our advice is: Don't worry! Just as children have different personalities, they also develop differently, depending upon their unique internal genetic clocks and the environment they're in.

Child development is defined as the noticeable milestones children accomplish as they learn and grow. The main types of development are physical, cognitive

(mental), social, language, and emotional. All of these are equally important and are rapidly occurring, but the most noticeable development is physical. Kids grow out of their clothing, lose their "baby fat," eat more, get taller and heavier, become coordinated, and learn to crawl, walk, and run. It's easy to see children's physical progress as they grow.

> Between 18 and 20 months, a child may learn ten or more new words a day.[1]

Cognitive development is the world of thought processing that is opening up to your child. He or she is becoming more aware of the world, beginning to see differences in people and things, and starting to use reasoning and judgment. Whenever your child asks *"Why?"* or can distinguish between a stranger and a friend, his or her cognitive processes are developing. Language development is a major part of cognitive development. Young children's communication begins with babbling and cooing. This is an essential first step toward being able to pronounce vowels and consonants and eventually the words that make language.

How your child relates to other people and gets along in the world are crucial development skills. This emotional and social development may include establishing feelings of well-being, attachment, and independence. All of these are important because they enable children to "connect" with others and to begin to understand that what they do can affect the people around them. Development in these areas also helps children learn how to make friends, cooperate, and express emotions.

Helpful Hints

As a parent, you may feel overwhelmed by the developmental responsibilities of rearing a child. And you may wonder how best to help your child develop in the areas we've discussed.

One powerful but simple answer is to spend time with your child. We mentioned this before, but cannot emphasize enough how important your attention is to that little person you're rearing. For example, something as simple as spending time playing with your kids will help them learn about how toys work, and how people communicate and cooperate when they are doing activities together. Or when you hug a child or smile or sing a song, you help him or her experience emotion – what it feels like to be loved and given attention. These are vital experiences in developing

> Babies dream half the time they are asleep, which is twice as much as adults dream.[1]

into happy, productive members of society. Read to a child and she begins to experience the magic of language. Show a child how to stack blocks and he starts to conceptualize how structures fit together. Play a game together and a child learns that cooperation is fun. Praise a child for stacking blocks and that child begins to feel pride in creation.

> By age 3, most children can understand most language they will use in ordinary conversation for the rest of their lives.[1]

While we don't recommend comparing your child's accomplishments with those of your siblings' children or the kids down the street, pediatricians and child-care experts have established developmental guidelines that illustrate some fundamental milestones that most youngsters reach by a certain age range.

On the next pages, you can review some of those milestones in the categories of physical, cognitive, emotional/ social, and language development. See where your child fits in. If you have concerns about his or her development, contact your pediatrician or family physician. Knowing what developmental milestones your children have reached affects what expectations you set for them. You will read more about setting reasonable expectations in an upcoming chapter.

Remember that children develop at different rates. Don't worry if your child reaches some milestones a couple of months later than a neighbor's child. Walking is a good example. On the average, children take their first steps when they are about 11 months old, but many children don't walk until they are 17 months old. Some kids walk as early as nine months old. As a general rule, you should not be concerned that your child is late in reaching a developmental milestone until he or she is six months past the average.

As you read the developmental charts, it may be very helpful to write down each development area and list the milestones your child has already accomplished. You will find that you become more focused and changes become more apparent. The child development charts also help you become aware of the next step in your child's growth.

[1] White, B.L. (1995). *The first three years of life.* New York: Simon and Schuster.

Birth to Six Months

How I Grow and Learn

"I am growing so fast! I am learning about the world in so many ways. I put most things in my mouth! My eyes can focus better now and my hearing is developing pretty well. I love to smile, coo, and babble at people who are familiar to me."

Physical – Rapid height and weight gain; gradually develops a sleep schedule for days and nights; holds head up, rolls over, and reaches for objects; can sit alone for short periods; may begin teething; puts anything he or she can grasp in mouth; uses motions that resemble crawling; may hold objects in both hands, but does not grasp them tightly; begins to hold a cup

Cognitive – Hearing is well developed by six months; reacts to others speaking native language; eyes focus clearly; recognizes bottle joyfully; plays with rattle

Language – Begins cooing, and is babbling by six months

Emotional/Social – May be afraid of unfamiliar people, but smiles and babbles socially with familiar people; raises arms to be picked up; expresses signs of almost all basic emotions (happiness, interest, surprise, fear, anger, sadness, disgust); can mimic adults' emotional expressions during face-to-face interactions; is curious about environment

Six Months to One Year

How I Grow and Learn

"I am getting more mobile! I can sit by myself and crawl. Some of my friends are walking, but I still hold on to the furniture, just in case! I know my name and I can say 'Mama' and 'Dada.' I love listening to music and I am learning to feed myself."

Physical – Sits alone, crawls, stands holding on to furniture, may walk; ability to grasp items between thumb and fingers improves; gives and takes objects; may favor using left hand or right hand

Cognitive – Recognizes name; enjoys listening to music; repeats chance behaviors that lead to fun or interesting results, such as a new noise; responds joyfully to image in mirror; can tell the difference between children and adults; engages in intentional or goal-directed behavior

Language – Loves to make noise; babbling expands to include sounds of spoken language; may repeat simple phrases; may say "Dada" or "Mama"; uses pointing or showing to communicate; understands a few words and may respond to short, simple requests; understands the meaning of "no"

Emotional/Social – May insist on feeding self; shows independence by not always being cooperative; begins trying to imitate parent behaviors; shows some fear of strangers; shows attachment to familiar caregivers; uses caregiver as a secure base for exploration; shows more frequent displays of anger and fear; smiles and laughs socially; shows very strong attachment to mother and develops attachment to father, siblings, and other familiar people

13 to 18 Months

How I Grow and Learn

"I am walking now. I like to explore and to imitate what I see. I am saying my first words and feeding myself. I like to spend time with Mommy and Daddy and play games like peek-a-boo. I am beginning to understand how to use things like my comb."

Physical – Rapid height and weight gain, but not as great as in first year; stands without help; walks without help with wide stance and outstretched arms; climbs stairs with help; may scribble with pencil; builds tower of two or three blocks, improves grasp; enjoys throwing, rolling, pushing, pulling toys; picks up objects from a standing position; loves water play; likes to feed self

Cognitive – Looks for hidden objects in last place the object was seen; begins to experiment through trial and error; begins to generalize behavior (e.g., uses behavior learned at day care when he or she is at home); shows more negativism; explores everything; begins to use more objects with purpose (e.g., comb in hair); likes to watch and imitate activities

Language – Adds gestures to speech; says first words; actively joins in taking turns, such as in pat-a-cake and peek-a-boo

Emotional/Social – Looks to parent for help in solving problems; prefers adults to other children; actively joins in play with siblings; recognizes images of self in mirrors and on videotape; shows signs of empathy; capable of compliance

18 to 24 Months

How I Grow and Learn

"I am walking better now. I can jump, run, and climb, but I take a lot of tumbles. I like to try feeding and dressing myself. I understand more words now, but you may think the only word I say is 'no.' I just like being more independent!"

Physical – Walks well; also jumps, runs, and climbs, but may fall a lot; manipulates objects with good coordination; builds tower of four or five blocks; enjoys pushing and pulling toys while walking; can walk backwards a short distance; may begin toilet training; begins to eat with a fork

Cognitive – Can find hidden objects; understands that something exists even though it is hidden; engages in make-believe play; is able to categorize objects more efficiently; can picture objects and events mentally; begins to develop a concept of himself or herself as a person; likes to show some independence (e.g., feeds self, undresses self); resists bedtime

Language – Can speak from 3 to 50 words, but may understand up to 200 words; wants to name everything; responds to simple requests; repeats familiar and unfamiliar sounds and gestures; responds with "no" often

Emotional/Social – Experiences beginnings of conscience with emotions such as shame and embarrassment; has a vocabulary of emotional terms and starts to use language to talk about emotions and feelings; begins to tolerate caregiver absences more easily; uses own name and personal pronoun to label image of self; categorizes self and others on the basis of age and sex; self-control appears; may favor father; enjoys imitating parents; may show strong attachment to toy or blanket

Two to Three Years

How I Grow and Learn

"I am much more coordinated than when I was younger. I understand more words and I can use more words. I like to have my own way and sometimes I get upset when my routine changes. I can use the toilet better by myself, but I still need some help."

Physical – Slower gains in height and weight than in toddlerhood; balance improves, walking becomes better coordinated; is able to run, jump, climb, hop, throw, and catch; can put on and remove some clothing; can button and unbutton large buttons; uses spoon effectively; constantly in motion; walks up and down stairs alone; begins to tiptoe; progresses from random scribbling to somewhat more controlled drawing; develops greater independence in toilet use, but still needs help; has difficulty settling down for bedtime

Cognitive – Can take the perspective of others in simple situations; is aware of the difference between inner thoughts and outer physical events; has difficulty making choices; can be difficult to reason with

Language – Vocabulary increases rapidly; can construct sentences that follow basic word order of native language; has some sense of grammar; displays effective conversational skills, such as taking turns and staying on a topic; shows independence by saying "no" regularly

Emotional/Social – Begins to develop self-concept; can distinguish between intentional and unintentional acts; begins to use cooperative behaviors; understands causes and consequences of basic emotions; shows increased understanding of others' feelings; knows gender; easily becomes upset or impatient; shows anger by crying or striking out; becomes frustrated when not understood; wants own way; reverts to baby behaviors at times; gets upset when daily routine changes; shows frequent mood changes; becomes more interested in brothers and sisters; may have an imaginary playmate; enjoys playing among, not with, other children; does not share and claims everything as his or her own; may scratch, hit, bite, and push other children

Three to Four Years

How I Grow and Learn

"Sometimes it seems that I am moving in all directions at once because I can hop and throw and catch now. I can skip on one foot and gallop. I am learning how to count and to name colors. I like to tell stories. Sometimes I cannot tell what is real and what's not, so I might worry that monsters are around me."

Physical – Running, jumping, hopping, throwing, and catching become better coordinated; can skip on one foot and gallop; moves forward and backward with agility; can ride a tricycle; kicks ball forward; throws ball overhand; can use safety scissors, draws first picture of a person

Cognitive – Notices when things change; can classify items; talks to himself or herself to guide behavior in challenging tasks; can remember and apply information he or she remembers from one situation to another; can count small numbers of objects; correctly names some colors; engages in make-believe play; begins to have a clearer sense of time

Language – Understands the concepts of "same" and "different"; has mastered some basic rules of grammar; speaks in sentences of five or six words; tells stories; can speak clearly enough that strangers understand

Emotional/Social – Is better able to control emotions; self-conscious emotions like shame, embarrassment, guilt, envy, and pride become more common; forms first friendships; ability to play with others improves; preference for same-sex playmates increases; plays "Mom" or "Dad"; imagines that many unfamiliar images may be "monsters"; often cannot distinguish between fantasy and reality

Five to Six Years

How I Grow and Learn

"I am growing taller and feeling more grown up because I'm getting my first permanent tooth. I can tie my shoes and draw pictures with more detail. I know a little about adding and subtracting and about how time works. I like to sing and dance. I want my friends to like me."

Physical – Body becomes more streamlined, with longer legs; can skip and stand on one foot for 10 seconds or longer; first permanent tooth comes in; gross motor skills increase in speed and endurance; ties shoes; writes name; knows some letters of the alphabet and can print them; usually cares for own toilet needs, dresses and undresses without assistance; can use fork, spoon, and sometimes a table knife

Cognitive – Ability to pay attention increases; improved ability to distinguish real images from imaginary images (e.g., knows person wearing a Halloween costume is not really a monster); memory improves; can do simple addition and subtraction; can count 10 or more objects; correctly names at least four colors; better understands the concept of time; knows about items used every day in the home (money, food, appliances)

Language – Speaks sentences of more than five words; uses future tense; says name and address; can tell longer stories; uses language to express empathy

Emotional/Social – Likes to sing, dance, and act; wants to please his or her friends and wants to be like those friends; more likely to agree to rules, but also can be demanding; shows more independence; understands basics about sex differences; able to distinguish fantasy from reality; better able to read social cues and to interpret, predict, and influence others' emotional reactions

Summing Up

Knowing some basic information about child development is an important part of improving your parenting skills. When you are aware of your children's abilities and what they can be expected to do at various ages, it can help you gear your teaching, discipline, and nurturing to fit their needs and developmental level. That way, you don't risk asking your child to do something he or she isn't able to do or set expectations that are too high. These situations can lead to frustration and discourage both you and your child. (We'll talk more about this in the next chapter.) Most importantly, determining where your child is in his or her physical, cognitive, emotional, and social development gives you a starting point for using the parenting methods we will talk about in this book.

Sources for child development milestones

Berk, L.F. (1996, 2012). *Infants, children, and adolescents.* Boston: Allyn & Bacon.

Developmental Milestones. (2014, March 27). Centers for Disease Control and Prevention. Retrieved July 31, 2014, from http://www.cdc.gov/NCBDDD/actearly/milestones/index.html

Manczak, D.W. (1986-1997). *Normal childhood development.* Greenwood Village, CO: National Health Enhancement Systems, Clinical Reference Systems, Ltd.

Shelov, S.P., & Hannemann, R.E. (1993, 2009). *Caring for your baby and young child: Birth to age 5.* New York: Bantam Books.

Be Reasonable!

Setting Expectations for Your Child

* *

A s you learn more about your child's development, you will be better able to identify reasonable expectations for his or her behaviors and accomplishments. Expectations frequently are a source of conflict between parents and children.

Often, we ask parents why they read our *Common Sense Parenting* books or take our *Common Sense Parenting* classes. They frequently answer that they want less conflict with their children. Usually this means they want their children to stop doing something negative or start doing something positive.

For example, parents say that they don't want their son to throw a fit when they tell him to pick up his toys. Instead, they do want him to say *"Okay"* and pick up the toys right away. Or they don't want their daughter to argue when she's told she can't have any candy at the grocery store. Instead, they do want her to calmly accept their *"No"* answers. These *Do's* and *Don'ts* are all examples of parents' expectations for their children's behavior. In this section, we will talk about these expectations: how to develop them, how to clarify them, and how to encourage improvements toward them.

Developing Clear Expectations

Our quick look at child development shows us that kids develop at their own unique pace and in their own unique ways. That means there are limits to what we can expect from children at all ages. For example, it would be reasonable to expect a 4-year-old to be able to dress herself with some help from you, such as showing her how to put on her clothing. She can probably handle a Velcro closure on her shoes, but she isn't likely to know yet how to tie her shoelaces. If she's had some coaching from you, dressing herself is a reasonable expectation, given the child's age, abilities, and resources.

Reasonable expectations are appropriate for a child's age, ability, and development. Having reasonable expectations for children is important because they make it easier for children to be successful and make parents feel less frustrated.

How do you know whether an expectation is reasonable or not? If you can answer *"Yes"* to all four of the following questions, then you are probably on your way to developing reasonable expectations for your children.

* **Have you taught the expectation to your children?**

In *Common Sense Parenting*, we describe how to teach your children the various skills they will need to be successful. Teach your children these skills and what you expect of them ahead of time. It is unreasonable to expect your kids to be able to do something if you haven't taught them how to do it.

> Common in children under age 5, "magical thinking" is the belief that one's thoughts or feelings influence people or the environment nearby and can trigger events.[1]

* **Can your children understand what you taught?**

One way to check for understanding is to have your children describe in their own words what you've said to them. Your child may not use your exact words, but the description will indicate whether your expectations were clear and whether he or she understands them.

✴ Can your children demonstrate what you taught?

Ask your children to show you what you have taught them. If they can demonstrate the task reasonably well, then your expectation is probably within your children's abilities.

✴ Have you modeled the behavior you want your children to do?

Do you routinely show your children what you want them to do? Modeling is a very important and very powerful learning tool; your children are always watching what you do and trying to imitate your behavior. So if you want your son to learn to throw a dirty sock in the hamper, let him see you do it and then have him repeat what you did by throwing another sock in the hamper. If you want your daughter to say *"Thank you"* when you give her a toy, tell her *"Thank you"* when she gives you something. Young children usually learn more by mimicking what you do than by listening to what you say.

Clarifying Expectations

There are two important parts of clarifying expectations for your kids. The first part involves what you say and the second part involves what you do. We will be discussing this in more detail later, but mention it here so you can begin thinking about it.

What you say.

Use short sentences and words your kids can understand. Also keep in mind that expectations are usually clearer and more effective when you describe them in a positive way, instead of telling your kids what not to do.

> The average 2½-year-old thinks that anything that moves is alive (moving automobile, rolling ball).

There still will be times when you use a *don't* statement, but try to follow it up with a *do* statement. For example, you might tell your 4-year-old, *"Don't draw on the wall."* You then should add, *"When you want to draw, ask me for some paper and sit at the table to draw."*

By positively describing your expectations, you clearly tell your child what he or she should do in the future. Always try to tell your child what you *do* want him or her to do, rather than simply saying what you *don't* want.

What you do.

How do you make sure your children understand your expectations? First, remember to model what you want your child to learn. In other words, practice what you preach. Children are more likely to learn your expectations from what they see you do rather than what you say. If you want your kids to say *"Please"* and *"Thank you,"* then you should consistently use those words. If you want your kids to tell the truth, let them see you being truthful in your dealings with others. Many times, actions really do speak louder than words. So be a consistent and positive role model. Your children will have a much clearer understanding of your expectations when you do.

After you have clearly explained and modeled your expectations, praise behaviors you see that are consistent with your expectations, and correct behaviors you see that don't meet those expectations.

For example, if your 5-year-old doesn't whine and ask for candy at the store as he has in the past, specifically tell him what he did right. Learn to always recognize positive behavior.

Likewise, if your child argues with you after you tell him *"No,"* correct his behavior. Specifically describe the behavior and then tell him what behavior you expect. Letting him argue and whine after you tell him "No" only teaches him to test your limits more and continue with the misbehavior.

If you hear yourself beginning to say things such as, *"If I have to tell you one more time,"* or *"Don't make me come in there,"* instead of specifically describing what you want, you are not giving your children clear expectations for how you want them to behave. You are, however, giving them a message that they have several more chances to misbehave because you're not going to immediately deal with their misbehavior. Clear expectations come from the consistent way you respond to your children's positive and negative behaviors.

> Louis XIV was crowned king of France at age 5.

Parents also need to agree on what expectations they have for their children. *All* parents need to have consistent expectations and methods of discipline. For some two-parent families, agreeing on expectations can be a problem. One parent may think the other is unreasonable, either too strict or too lax. It takes constant effort and good communication for two parents who may have different approaches to parenting to set expectations they can both agree on. Parents must learn to negotiate with one another. It also is important for them to agree not to argue about expectations in front of the kids. When parents can't agree, it makes life confusing and problematic for everyone in the family. It's worth the effort for both parents to develop similar expectations for their children's behavior. In the long run, setting clear expectations benefits everyone in the family.

In addition, parents need to look at the expectations they have for themselves. Sometimes, it's difficult for parents of very young children to adjust to the demands of parenthood. They may find it hard to keep up with the increased workload of laundry and the 1,001 other tasks that are part of caring for a young child.

Or, they miss the leisure time they enjoyed when they didn't have children and adult activities like dining out regularly or seeing the latest movies. When kids come along, parents have to cut back on their social life, and that can require a big adjustment.

Here are some questions to ask yourself about your expectations of family life: Have you done an expectation "check" lately? Do you need to readjust your expectations of how much time being a good parent will take? Do you need to plan some regular time away from your children, such as a monthly "adults' night out"?

Summing Up

Clear expectations help children understand what they should and shouldn't do. They provide a framework for positive behavior. Even though kids won't meet your expectations all the time, consistency and patience will pay off in the long run. Remember to ask yourself four important questions:

"Have I taught what I expect?"

"Can my children understand what I taught?"

"Can my children demonstrate what I expect?"

"Have I modeled what I want my children to do?"

If you can answer *"Yes"* to these questions, you're doing a great job of setting clear and reasonable expectations.

Remember that parents' expectations for themselves also are important. Take time regularly to assess what your expectations are in all aspects of your life – parenting, social life, career, community involvement, etc.

---

[1] Franck, I., & Brownstone, D. (1996). *Parenting A to Z.* New York: Harper Collins.

Frequently Asked Questions
about

Reasonable Expectations

  "What can I expect when it comes to my child's ability to play nicely with other children?"

You can expect children ages 2 to 5 to initially have trouble playing well with others. It's very common for some children not to learn how to share until they are 3 or 4. They still believe that everything is "mine." They may enjoy being together with other children at times but they're not yet ready to handle all of the newness of relationships. Be sure to use *Effective Praise* (see Chapter 7) when you do see your child playing nicely with other kids. Children often learn play behaviors by imitating other children, especially an older sibling. Eventually, children will begin to share certain objects and learn to cooperate during playtime.

  "My daughter bullies other kids. Is that normal behavior, and what should I do about it?"

Some bullying is to be expected from kids as part of normal development. But if the bullying becomes frequent, teach a positive replacement behavior. Several times each day, have your daughter practice ways to be considerate of others. Teach her how to cooperate and get things in a socially acceptable way. Allow her to earn fun things when she practices or interacts well with others. Give negative consequences for any bullying behaviors you see your child do. Use a firm, no-nonsense voice tone and don't use any bullying behaviors yourself.

 "My 3-year-old has recently started clinging to me whenever I try to go somewhere without him. Is this normal? Is there something I can do?"

 The answer is yes to both questions. Around eight months old, children begin to develop a sense of who they are and who their parents are. Clinging can be part of the bonding process between a parent and child. As children grow older, they may continue to cling to a parent because of the security they feel. To encourage independence in your child, give him small tasks that you know he can accomplish and praise him for playing alone or with others. Practice with your child what he should do when you have to leave the home. Set up positive consequences for not clinging to you. Keep in mind that it may take your child a while to feel secure and independent, and that some whining or crying is to be expected, so be patient.

It's Child's Play!

Ways to Nurture Your Child

* *

One of the most important qualities of good parenting is nurturing your children. Nurturing means showing your children they are loved and accepted so that they can grow and develop. Many kinds of behaviors can be nurturing: smiles, hugs, kisses, words of encouragement, a soothing backrub, making a favorite meal, listening – any action that shows your child that you love him or her.

A good way to remember to use nurturing behaviors is to think of the acronym **SCALE:**

S: Support – *Providing children with physical and emotional support*

C: Caring – *Showing affection for children through everyday actions like preparing nutritious meals and ensuring that they have sufficient sleep*

A: **Acceptance** – *Showing unconditional love*

L: **Love** – *Displaying physical and emotional attachment (appropriate to the child's age and developmental level)*

E: **Encouragement** – *Offering children hope, courage, and confidence*

Remember to use the **SCALE** to balance nurturing behaviors with teaching and discipline. That's the best way for healthy child development to occur. It's the balance of the *heart* and *head* that we talked about in the first part of this book.

For some parents, using nurturing behaviors is second nature. They find it easy to communicate to their children and others how they feel. They know just when to offer a smile or a hug and when just to be a good listener.

Other parents may find nurturing tougher. Maybe they don't believe they're very good at showing their feelings, or they find it difficult to know what to say in certain situations.

Whatever your situation is, learn what techniques work with your kids, and use those nurturing behaviors to help create a solid foundation for their growth. The key is to develop a relationship with your child that is rooted in honesty and love.

Let's look more closely at some of the vital signs of relationships, the elements that make a relationship vibrant and worthwhile. You probably possess many of these qualities now. If so, maybe you'll find ways to enhance what you already have. Maybe thinking about these qualities will help you discover new ways to make the most of your nurturing potential. Take some time to select a few skills you can learn, and make this part of your goal for personal improvement. Let's face it – if we all don't continually strive for improvement, the stresses of life tend to push us back into old habits. Then, negative behaviors can surface out of our frustrations.

> "If you want your children to be intelligent, read them fairy tales. If you want them to be more intelligent, read them more fairy tales."
>
> —*Albert Einstein*

It is a good bet that making the following qualities part of your personality will help you nurture happy and healthy relationships with everyone. They will be especially useful as you teach your kids to live happier, richer lives.

Play

Playing with your kids is more than just fun and games. It's a special time to fuel imagination, build skills, explore, and most of all, be together.

Play is an important part of how children overcome challenges, develop their minds and bodies, and learn to get along with others. When you take time to join in play – throwing balls, stacking blocks, and attending tea parties – you help your children learn those life skills. You also learn more about your child's abilities and how he or she sees the world. There's another benefit too – it's fun!

In this next section, we will review how parents can become good playmates, how games can help children face challenges, and how playtime activities can teach children powerful life lessons.

Playing Together

Sometimes, parents try too hard when they play with their kids. Instead of playing, they spend time correcting the kids or showing them how they would do something. *"No, honey. That block goes on top,"* they say, or *"Wait. Let me do that for you."* It's okay to set certain expectations such as not throwing things or writing on walls, of course, but don't suppress the fun of playing by constantly giving instructions or criticism.

If you want to have more fun playing with your child, let him or her take the lead at playtime. After all, children are the experts when it comes to play. Here are some other tips for being a better playmate:

Learn to enjoy playing.

Don't bring work to the pleasure of play. Relax and give yourself and your children permission to have fun. Don't be a clock-watcher during playtime. Try to devote yourself entirely to your child when you're playing together and don't worry about other things you might have to do. Ask yourself if an extra five minutes of playtime is really going to prohibit you from getting your other work done. The most important commitment you have is the child right in front of you with a stack of blocks or a soccer ball.

Be creative.

Don't get stuck on store-bought stuff. Some of the best games in the world are free of charge. There are lots of creative and inventive ways to play with your children. Whether it's exploring an anthill, building sand castles, or just taking a walk, there are lots of opportunities for cultivating young imaginations, especially in the great outdoors. Spark your child's creativity and problem-solving ability by asking questions as you play, or ask your child to pretend he or she is someone – or something – else, such as an animal.

Take the role you're given.

When your child assigns you a role during playtime, be a good sport and follow the script. If he wants to be the daddy and you to be the child in the pretend game, so be it. Pretending to be someone else is a great way for children to learn how others think and feel.

> "But a group of toddlers making up a story together is a much richer learning experience than dragging things across a screen to make a story. Children learn best in the context of relationships."
>
> — *Claire Lerner*

Limit watching television and other 'screen time' as a form of play.

Watching an occasional video or television program with your child, or playing a game on the computer together, can be a great way to relax, but don't let the TV or the computer become your main sources of play or a baby-sitter for your kids. In addition, make sure you interact with your children when you do watch videos or television programs together. Let the program content provide you with opportunities to offer explanations, share opinions, or talk to your kids about values. Many videos and programs are educational as well as entertaining. You just have to make sure you are in control of the television set and the computer, and not vice-versa. Set a limit on how much television your children may watch.

Make time to play.

Don't expect your children to invite you to play. Parents sometimes subtly give their children the impression they are not available for playing, so children may try to get their parents' attention in inappropriate ways. Taking the initiative to make time to play with your children lets them know you care and are available. Children want to know they are special to their parents. These play dates don't need to be long. In fact, having several short playtimes during the day is usually better for everyone. Some examples of when to enjoy playtime might be after meals or chores, or for a few minutes when everyone arrives home.

The Importance of Play

Different types of play teach children different life lessons. Here's a quick look at how important play is:

Physical Play

Physical play – running, jumping, climbing, squeezing, squashing, throwing, and catching – helps children hone their fine motor skills. Through physical play, children learn how they can use their minds and bodies to manipulate their world.

Running, jumping, and other forms of active play, especially team sports, also help increase kids' confidence in their bodies and teach them how to cooperate with others and work toward a common goal.

Imagination and Pretending

Encourage your children to play with toys that spark their imagination, such as blocks, dolls, stuffed animals, action figures, or household items. Toys that encourage kids to use their imagination help them learn creativity and problem-solving, two skills that come in mighty handy as children grow.

A pile of blocks, for example, can become anything a child might imagine – a giant castle, or maybe a spaceship. Household items also can become awesome imaginary tools. A wooden spoon might be a magic wand, and an old blanket makes a great play tent.

Sharing and Communication Play

Some board games and children's games like tag or hide-and-seek can help children learn how to communicate and cooperate by taking turns and being part of a team. Check out your local bookstore for a book on children's games.

Drawing and doing craftwork helps children learn how to express themselves or share their feelings. Singing games also help children understand how words represent different objects.

Playtime Suggestions

Here are some examples of fun games you can play with your children:

Name Game: Help your children learn to describe objects, people, and things using words. Have a word of the day, such as "round." (Example: Look around the house and find as many round things as possible. Talk about round items you see as you drive to day care or preschool.) Try to use the word with different objects, things, and people you and your children encounter during the day. This is a great way to increase your child's vocabulary and understanding of how to use words.

Sock Puppet Show: Have your children tell stories using their imagination and an old sock as a puppet. Children can learn to express their feelings and thoughts with the puppet. Help your children create an animal or some other imaginary creature out of the sock using yarn, felt, patches of cloth, etc. Each night at bedtime, the puppet and your child can tell you what happened to him or her that day. Or, you can use the sock puppet and tell your child a story.

Cut and Paste: Supervise your children as they learn to use scissors and paste paper together. Make greeting cards, pictures to send to grandparents, and other colorful works of art. Let your children express their feelings while improving their fine motor skills.

Note: Safety is important here. Supervise, teach, and make sure sharp scissors aren't easily accessible when you're not around.

Dress-Up and Pretend: Provide old clothes to help your children try out new roles. Ask your children questions about the person they are pretending to be, such as what the person does for a living or where the person lives.

Finger Paints: Give your children large paper grocery bags with a hole cut in the bottom and let them use finger paints to draw an object, animal, or plant. Once the paint dries, let them put on their creation and demonstrate what that thing does, how it might be feeling, or how people could use it.

Water Balloon Toss: This helps your children develop hand-eye coordination and their ability to interact with others. On a hot summer day, a water balloon toss is a great way to cool off and work on upper-body flexibility and other physical skills.

Musical Chairs: Teach your children to appreciate music while playing a fun game with chairs and music. The game works best with several children. Arrange several folding chairs or kitchen chairs in a row. Have one less chair than there are players. Tell the children they will be walking around the chairs as music plays. The object of the game is to sit down on a chair without hurting others when the music stops. The person who does not have a seat when the music stops is out of the game. You can use a musical instrument, radio, CD player, or iPod for your music source. You may want to briefly discuss with the children the instrument or music they heard after the game is over.

Picture Time: Catch your children being good. Take a picture of them in the act of playing nicely, putting their toys away, or reading a book. Put the picture up in a place of honor.

> The game of tug-of-war is 4,000 years old.

Sticker Fun: Use stickers to help encourage positive play. When your child is getting along with others, put a sticker on his or her shirt as a reward for positive behavior. This way, everyone will see he or she has been good.

My Little Helper: Young children love to help out around the house. Provide your children with safe things they can do with your help and guidance.

On the next page is a list of tasks that are developmentally appropriate for young children and will give you some ideas to get started. These tasks give you a way to begin teaching your young children about responsibility, helping others, and being part of a family. Having children involved in tasks around the house can also help them grow in various developmental areas.

Chores for Young Children

Ages 3-4

Clean up spills

Pick up toys

Wipe off part of a table

Set plates, utensils, cups on a table (use unbreakable items)

Match socks

Put clothing in hamper

Pour dry cereal

Rinse items in sink (fruits, vegetables, unbreakable dishes)

Stir pancake batter

Shut off TV or lights

Pour pet food in bowl

Put folded clothes in a drawer

Hold a door open for others

Carry items in from the car (small items and unbreakables)

Clear meal items from the table (unbreakables and items that won't spill)

Ages 5-6

All chores from the list for 3- and 4-year-olds

Straighten blankets on bed

Fold towels

Learn to handle table knife

Load clothes into dryer

Find items in the supermarket

Prepare simple snacks (spread butter or jelly on bread)

Dust furniture

Vacuum

Water plants

Organize items on a shelf (toys, books, unbreakables)

Help with younger siblings (bring a diaper or toy, share toys, look at book together)

Rinse things with hose (car, sidewalk, bicycle)

Hold dustpan

Pour water in pet dish

Fold shirts or pants

Humor

Having a good sense of humor is an invaluable nurturing tool for parents. When you laugh at silly jokes with your kids and encourage them to find humor in the world around them, things just seem to go better. When you show your children that you have a good sense of humor, you help teach them how healthy it is to laugh. Remember, kids need a break from their stresses just as much as adults do!

Humor brings perspective. Being a parent is full of ups and downs. If you don't learn how to find humor in what happens, you will constantly dwell on all the bad things. A good sense of humor can insulate you from negative feelings that can get the best of you and hinder your efforts to teach your kids.

You don't have to be a stand-up comedian to use humor. The point is to communicate to your children that you see the funny side of life. With small children, you can have fun making funny faces or using funny voices. Maybe you're a good storyteller and like to get a laugh through the tall tales you tell. Perhaps your sense of humor leans more toward the use of exaggeration and understatement, and you can bring a smile to your kids' faces with remarks like *"He must have eaten a bazillion tacos."*

Whatever method you use, it's important to make your humor a natural extension of your personality. Used in this way, humor provides welcome relief from the everyday stresses of life and allows us to relax and enjoy each other.

Encourage your children's attempts at humor, and teach them about when to use it and when not to use it. Emphasize that humor is never to be used to belittle another person or when someone makes a mistake or gets hurt. Humor lifts people up; it doesn't put them down. When your children are very young, be mindful that you may reinforce a behavior if you laugh at it. Don't laugh at something you don't want to see again, like spitting out food.

Empathy

Empathy means trying to understand another person's situation and feelings. For many people – parents included – this is not easy. Many of us grew up being told what we should do and how we should feel. In fact, many of us may even have been taught to deny our true feelings. We heard statements like *"You don't really mean that"*; *"Shake it off. It's no big deal"*; or *"There's no reason to feel that way. Straighten up and fly right."* Our parents probably made statements like these to us, and we may find ourselves saying the same things to our kids.

But being a parent with empathy means resisting the urge to just do things the way they've always been done. We have to go a step further, and try, as much as possible, to see the world as our kids see it and feel the world as they feel it. Only then can we begin to help them make sense of the world, which is our responsibility as parents.

Being the parent of a very young child can test our abilities to empathize. Sometimes, we have to work hard to recall what it was like when we were children. It's easy to forget how hard it is to communicate when you don't know all the words you need, how difficult it is to eat without getting messy, and how confusing it is when you want to explore and people keep telling you *"No!"*

> "Each day of our lives we make deposits in the memory banks of our children."
>
> – *Charles Swindell*

For young children, life is a constant discovery, and you must be understanding so you don't dampen their enthusiasm for learning. You also must try to understand their frustrations and fears.

Keep those ideas in mind the next time you grow frustrated with your toddler or preschooler. Use empathy and look at the situation from your child's perspective. Think about your expectations for your child and whether he or she is able to meet them. What does your child need to know to more successfully handle the situation? In short, stop, think, and then teach.

Praise

Praise is nourishment. It helps children grow emotionally just as food helps them grow physically. Praising your children's good behaviors and even their not-quite-successful efforts at good behavior is important.

At Boys Town, we believe that praise is such an important part of parenting that we have developed a type of teaching called *Effective Praise*. *Effective Praise* is a form of intentional praise. We'll talk more about *Effective Praise* in Chapter 7, as well as the different types of praise you can use to reinforce your children's behaviors. For now, let's look at some general guidelines for using praise:

* **Praise a child's behavior in a way the child can understand it.** Avoid using general phrases. Be specific about what the youngster did that you want him or her to do again. For example, say, *"You did a good job of washing your hands, Shante. You used soap and made a good lather. Your hands are really clean now!"*

* **Be brief.** Too much praise sounds phony, even to young children. Simply state the behavior in age-appropriate, specific, and understandable words.

* **Be enthusiastic!** Praise must have some emotion behind it. You should feel good that your child has met your expectations. Show it!

* **Give praise immediately (or as soon as you can).** Delayed praise loses its power to increase the likelihood that a child will use the positive behavior again. Immediacy is especially important with young children, for their worlds are all about the present. They won't remember what it was they did if you tell them they were good yesterday.

* **Don't dilute praise by referring to past inappropriate behaviors.** For example, avoid saying something like *"You picked up your toys! Wonderful! Why can't you do that all the time? Yesterday I had to ask you three times to pick up your toys."*

Summing Up

All of the nurturing behaviors we discussed can help your child grow and develop. These behaviors cultivate young minds and begin teaching them how to handle the fascinating new world opening up around them. Most importantly, nurturing your child brings you closer together, lets your child know that you love and care about him or her, and helps strengthen the relationship that is essential if your teaching is to be effective.

Frequently Asked Questions
about
Nurturing and Playing

"What's the best way to play with my child?"

Follow your child's lead when it comes to playing. Let him choose what to play with. Don't give too many instructions or commands. Praise good play behavior and set up some positive consequences for cooperating or sharing. There will be times when you have to correct him, so gently but firmly redirect him. At times, you can also take a break or ignore his behavior until he begins playing appropriately again. When he does play well, enjoy!

"Why is quantity of time more important than quality of time?"

The answer is simple: Parenting takes time. To be effective parents, we need to take advantage of all the time we have with our kids. We can't be a parent only when we feel like it. We have to have good relationships with our kids, and relationships take time to develop and grow. With all of the other responsibilities you have, there will be times when it would be easy to let parenting take a back seat. Don't allow that to happen. Use all of the techniques you learn in *Common Sense Parenting* to nourish the good times and diminish the bad times. You will have to make some sacrifices in your own life, but raising happy and responsible children should be a just reward.

  "What can my child learn during playtime?"

Many social skills can be learned from playing. Children can learn to share, cooperate with others, be creative, and be a good sport. You can practice some social skills by playing games. For example, kids can learn to follow instructions in "Simon Says," accept "No" and ask permission in "Mother May I?", or accept consequences in "Duck, Duck, Goose" or "Musical Chairs." Playtime can be valuable learning time.

  "Is it okay for my son to play with dolls?"

It's not unusual for young boys and girls to want to play with all kinds of different toys. There is no harm in that. In fact, parents should offer a full range of toys and encourage a variety of activities so their child can be socially well-rounded. Parents are the ones who view toys as gender-specific. Kids don't think that way; to kids, toys are simply toys.

4

Show and Tell

Your Role as a Teacher

* *

As parents, we are our children's first teachers. It is up to us to teach our youngsters the skills they need to function not only in our families but in society as well. Becoming a good teacher to children is a round-the-clock job because we're responsible for teaching kids everything from manners and morals to how to make scrambled eggs. That responsibility might seem overwhelming, but think about the wonderful opportunity it presents – whenever we are with our children, we have the opportunity to teach them something.

When we talk about being a parent, we inevitably talk about the time investment parenting takes. You must spend time with your kids to be a good parent.

As you think about the time you spend with your kids, your first thoughts probably will be about the good times you share with them, like family outings or a special birthday celebration. But sometimes, when your children misbehave, for example, you will have to spend time disciplining them, and that is difficult for many parents.

Parents often think about how they were disciplined when they were kids. To many, that might have meant a spanking or some other type of punishment.

> "A good parent remembers what it was like to be a child."
>
> – Anna Quindlen

But discipline really should be more about teaching than punishment. We discipline our children so they will learn how to live well with others and do the right thing. If you begin to think about discipline as a way to teach your children, then the situations in which you use discipline become opportunities to enhance your time together, rather than obstacles to your relationship.

Think about these ideas the next time you must correct your child's behavior. Rather than just focusing on what he or she did wrong, use the opportunity to teach your child how to make a better choice next time.

For example, if your son whines and asks for candy in the grocery store, teach him how to ask politely and accept *"No"* if that is the answer he receives. Remember, if you don't *teach* your child what's right, you can't expect him or her to *do* what's right.

It's easy to remember this idea of positive discipline if you keep these four concepts in mind:

T: **Teach** *your children by what you do and what you say.*

I: **Instruct** *them clearly in all areas of their lives.*

M: **Monitor** *what they do and how they do it.*

E: **Encourage** *them in failures as well as successes.*

You can easily remember these four concepts – Teach, Instruct, Monitor, and Encourage – by using the acronym **TIME.** Being a good parent means spending **TIME** with your children.

Positive Discipline = TIME

Keep in mind that just because we're talking about discipline as a type of teaching, we're not saying that kids shouldn't experience consequences for their inappropriate behaviors. That, too, is part of learning. We'll discuss consequences and how to effectively use them later in this book.

In the next section, we'll talk about another essential element of good parenting – communication.

Clear Communication

Like love, communication binds families together. When we communicate clearly and effectively with each other, we strengthen our family relationships, ease one another's frustrations, and create a place where everyone feels needed and successful.

But many times when we think about communicating with our kids, we think about things like telling them to pick up clothes, or put away toys, or quit jumping on the couch.

Sometimes we forget the simple things like asking them how they are, or giving them a hug when they wake up, or using the nurturing behaviors that we discussed earlier.

Here are some ideas that will help you communicate better with your young children.

Look and listen.

Since small children do not have an extensive vocabulary or the verbal skills to tell us how they're thinking and feeling, we have to use a variety of techniques to understand what they want us to know and to communicate with them.

Watch for the facial expressions and body language young kids use to communicate. You know the grimace your son makes when you feed him something he doesn't like. And when your daughter points to the refrigerator, you know she wants juice. Your child will communicate in a variety of nonverbal ways. Make sure you use facial expressions and body language, too. Smile, nod your head, and point at items and name them so your child begins to understand what things are called.

Be alert for early attempts at speaking and using words, and encourage them. If your daughter points to a ball and says *"Ba,"* you can say, *"Yes, that's a ball! You're right!"* You also can encourage speech development by listening to your kids. Respond enthusiastically to babbling, and talk back as if you understood every word. Don't interrupt your kids. Let them tell you their story. Ask questions to get them to tell you more. The skill of listening cannot be overemphasized. Listening demonstrates caring, interest, and warmth.

Choose the right time to communicate.

You can and should talk to your child anytime. But the best time to communicate is when you have enough time to focus on what you want to talk about. Don't try to have an important conversation with your child when you're late for work in the morning. Choose another time instead. Also, remember that effective communication won't happen if you or your child is angry or upset. The best interactions happen when everyone is calm.

Use your child's name or nickname.

It may sound simple, but frequently using your child's name makes communication more personal and meaningful. Some parents seem to reserve their child's first name only for correction. It's much better to use a child's name often so he or she develops a sense of identity. You might also use endearing terms like "Honey" or "Sweetheart" or a cute nickname when talking to your child. These are nice ways to nurture children.

Toddlers spend 12% to 17% of their waking hours simply staring. By age 3, they have cut their staring time by more than half.[1]

Talk face-to-face.

People communicate better when they can look one another in the eye. When you're talking with your child, make sure you have face-to-face conversations. Avoid across-the-room conversations or trying to talk to your child when you're in different rooms; that usually results in yelling. One exception is when you are driving and your child is in a car seat or is buckled up in the seat behind you. You can still talk to your child, but for safety's sake, you won't be able to be face-to-face.

Remove distractions.

If you have something really important to talk about with your child, do it in a place where you won't be disturbed. Shut off your phone or the television, or remove whatever other distraction might be interfering, and then talk. The same goes when your child wants to talk to you;

put down the paper or briefly stop whatever you're doing and listen attentively.

Get on your child's level.

Imagine talking to someone who is triple your size. It would have to be frightening. Don't put that kind of distance between you and your child. When you want to communicate, get down on the floor with him or her, sit on chairs facing one another, or curl up together on the couch.

These are ways to set the stage for communication to take place. But there are also some ways to help your child listen to what you say, especially when you are trying to teach and/or discipline him or her. Here are some tips:

Use simple words.

Use descriptive, uncomplicated words that a child can understand. Also, avoid using words that might be judgmental (calling a child a "brat").

Vague: *"You are throwing a fit!"*

Specific: *"You are crying and stomping your feet."*

Be brief.

Use short instructions to explain or redirect your child's behavior.

Wordy: *"What do you think you're doing? You're in big trouble! If you don't stop that this minute, you're going to be grounded for the rest of the year!"*

Brief: *"Stop jumping on the couch. For jumping on the couch, go to Time-Out."*

Be aware of your physical actions.

How you say something to a child can be even more important than what you say. For example, be firm and matter-of-fact when you are correcting misbehavior, but be animated and enthusiastic when you are communicating approval or just having fun with your child.

Don't: *Point your finger or stand over your child*

Do: *Get down to the child's level, relax your body, and avoid raising your voice or your hand*

Don't get sidetracked.

When your child wants to argue, don't respond. Keep the conversation focused on the initial topic.

Getting sidetracked: *"No, I'm not mean. Don't say 'I hate you.' It makes me sad."*

Staying focused: *"Jennifer, stop talking and listen to me."*

Avoid argument cycles.

Abruptly discontinue quarrels or disputes by walking away or taking time to calm down. Talk later when you and your child are both calm.

Argumentative: *"I'm sick of your constant complaining. If you'd just listen...."*

Calming: *"You are angry now and so is Mommy. Let's take some deep breaths to feel better. Then we can talk."*

Reframe negative statements.

Use verbal modeling to show your child how you want him or her to say something in a positive way.

Negative: *"Calling someone names is not nice!"*

Positive: *"I know that you are upset. Just say, 'I am mad.'"*

Demonstrate affection and empathy.

Use appropriate touch, smiles, winks, or statements of understanding to decrease problem behaviors and encourage positive steps toward good behavior.

Sarcastic: *"Why can't you act your age?"*

Empathetic: *"I understand it's hard, but I know you can do it!"* (smile)

Before we leave the topic of communication, let's talk briefly about how children develop communication and language skills.

As we discussed in the first chapter, children's language skills follow a developmental pattern, much like their physical and cognitive skills. Language develops gradually, starting with cooing and babbling when children are a few months old. By the time most kids reach age 5, they understand about 90 percent of the words adults use.

> "The mother's heart is the child's schoolroom."
>
> – Henry Ward Beecher

This means parents can't rely solely on words to communicate with their children when they are very young. Some language researchers advocate using more gestures, enhanced voice tones, and facial expressions with young children to improve communication. Also, demonstrate the behaviors you want your child to use.

For example, with a young child, you might point to the door and say, *"Let's go outside and play!"* or you might use your hands to mimic how a book opens and say enthusiastically, *"Let's read a story."* With an older child, you might say, *"Here's what you should say when you want something,"* and then say exactly what you want your child to say.

Keys to Clear Communication

Below are some key points to remember when you want to communicate clearly:

* **Be a good example.** Children are great imitators of adult behavior. Make sure to give children many good examples to follow.

* **Be brief and specific.** The attention span of young children is short; make sure your message is as brief as possible.

* **Be consistent.** Consistently showing and telling behavior can help children make positive changes more quickly.

* **Tell the *do's*.** Focus on the positive. Tell your children what they have done well or what you want them to do well. At times, you will also explain what was done incorrectly, but the focus should always be on doing better.

* **Mean what you say and say what you mean.** Avoid making idle threats or giving warnings. Even young children know when their parents mean what they say. Following through on what you say can help children learn not to push limits.

Describing Behaviors: Show and Tell

The first step toward better communication with your children is learning how to describe their behaviors to them, so you will be able to praise the wonderful things they're doing and start correcting those not-so-wonderful things.

Behaviors are anything our children say or do that can be seen or heard. Our job as parents is to pay more attention to those behaviors and then use a process we call *"Show and Tell"* to teach kids the skills we want them to learn.

Show and Tell sounds like a children's game, but it really is a very serious way to improve kids' behavior using everyday skills. In *Show and Tell*, you **use simple, concise words to describe behavior** to a child so the child will know whether the behavior is right or wrong. Essentially, you become a mirror so the child can see whether his or her behavior is acceptable.

For example, your 2-year-old throws her empty paper cup on the ground at the park. You pick up the cup, look at the child, and say, *"Emily, no. Your cup goes in the trash, not on the ground.* (Walk the child over to the trash receptacle and let her throw away the cup.) *There you go! Throw your cup in the trash when you're finished with it."*

With this simple dialogue, which uses some repetition to get the point across, you show and tell your child what the proper behavior is.

The trick to effectively using *Show and Tell* is to be very precise in describing behaviors. A good way to begin your descriptions is by saying, *"You just..."* or *"I heard you say...."* That way, your child will connect his or her actions with what you're saying.

Here are some examples of *Show and Tell*:

"You just pushed your brother and called him a baby."

Thank you for putting your toys in the toy box."

When I gave you the candy, you said 'Thank you.'"

"I want you to walk across the room without running."

Say 'Okay' when I say 'No.' Great! You said 'Okay.'"

Remember that *Show and Tell* is a tool to teach new skills, praise behaviors, or help stop behaviors while they're small – before they escalate. Look at what your child is doing and ask yourself what behavior is getting in the way of him or her doing what you want. Then describe that inappropriate behavior.

For example, if your son is playing with his blocks instead of picking them up like you asked, say, *"Jamel, you're still playing with your blocks. Please stop playing and put them in the toy box."*

Often, children will correct their behavior when you use *Show and Tell* to describe what they're doing wrong. But sometimes they will test the limits you set by continuing to behave inappropriately. When this happens, you must tell them they have earned a consequence for their continued inappropriate behavior. (In the next chapter, we'll explain consequences and how to use them in your teaching.)

> At 19 months, toddlers begin to understand when things don't conform to adult ideas. They'll laugh at something that is obviously wrong – like calling a dog a cat.

Remember, the more specific you can be in describing your child's behavior, the better. We all tell our kids *"Be good"* or *"You're a big girl,"* but kids often don't know what we mean. It's more effective to tell them exactly what you mean. If "being good" means not asking for candy at the store, then communicate that to your child. If "being a big girl" means asking for something only once and saying *"Okay,"* tell your child that.

You also might have to demonstrate behaviors in order to show and tell your kids what they need to know. One father we know asked his son to stop whining several times before the boy said, *"Daddy, I don't know what whining is."* So, the father appropriately demonstrated what the boy looked like and sounded like when he was whining, giving the child a better idea of the inappropriate behavior he was supposed to stop doing.

Show and Tell works because it helps you to specifically describe what the child is doing rather than focus on how you are reacting to that behavior. That's a great leveler for some of the emotion-packed parenting situations we find ourselves in.

Show and Tell also helps you avoid yelling or raising your voice to get your kids to listen to you. We all know that yelling and talking louder may work the first time, but if you use it repeatedly, your kids get conditioned to it and don't respond. That forces you to yell louder, which doesn't really solve the problem.

When you use *Show and Tell* to describe behaviors, it allows you to calmly and clearly communicate with your children. *Show and Tell* also improves your ability to be consistent and pleasant, and helps you develop a more effective parenting style.

Summing Up

Teaching our children is a vital part of parenting. In this section, we looked at a variety of skills we can use in our teaching:

Communication: How we talk to our kids and listen to what they have to say is a critical skill. We should remember concepts such as talking face-to-face, removing distractions, and getting on the same level with our children. We also should choose simple words to communicate successfully, and remember to be aware of our physical actions and gestures when we communicate with our children. Also, we should keep in mind our children's developmental levels; some very young children will understand better when adults use gestures and enhanced facial expressions.

Show and Tell: When you show and tell your children the behaviors they should use, you help them understand what skills they need to get along in the world. Remember to be very specific in describing and demonstrating behaviors for your children.

Remember that positive discipline takes **TIME** – Teach, Instruct, Monitor, and Encourage. Spending **TIME** with your children and helping them to learn the skills they need is the key to successful parenting.

---

[1] White, B.L. (1995). *The first three years of life.* New York: Simon and Schuster.

Frequently Asked Questions
about
Clear Communication

Q **"I ask my child a thousand times to do something and he never does what I ask him to do. How is clear communication going to help me?"**

A Clear communication will help you avoid sidetracks, argument cycles, and power struggles with your child. Describe the behavior you see or hear him doing. If he ignores you and continues to play, describe those behaviors to him. ("You're ignoring me; please stop playing and listen to me.") When you get his attention, calmly but firmly give him a clear instruction for what you want him to do. ("Let's pick up your toys. It's time to eat dinner.")

Q **"Can my 4-year-old really understand everything I say to her?"**

A Young children are capable of understanding many concepts. However, what they understand best are simple, concrete words and phrases. Therefore, it's important to show her what you want as well as use words to describe it. Understanding comes from frequently using a behavior and seeing the results of that behavior. That takes time, and a child's understanding develops gradually. Parents should consistently use *Show and Tell* and give children reasons for why they should behave a certain way.

"I have five children. Should I talk to them all together or separately when I'm trying to correct them?"

 It really depends on how comfortable you feel talking to them in a group and how well they listen to you when they are together. If things get too hectic when you try to talk with them together, talk to them one-on-one. You can work your way up to talking to them as a group. Setting up consequences in advance (see Chapter 5) will give you a consistent way of dealing with your kids if all of them are acting up at the same time. That way, they will know what will happen if they continue to misbehave.

 "My son is easily distracted and can hardly sit still for any instructions. What should I do?"

 Before you start talking, eliminate any distractions and make sure you have your child's attention. Get down on his eye level and use words he will understand. Because he has difficulty sitting still, keep whatever you say simple and brief.

 "My son doesn't take anything I say seriously. What should I do?"

 Let your son know when you are serious and when you are joking. Young children will not always know the difference. When you are serious, mean what you say and say what you mean. Young children respect actions more than words. Make sure you follow through on what you tell him. Make sure your voice tone, facial expressions, and body language give your son the correct message.

5

Cause and Effect

Using Consequences to Change Behavior

* *

Effective parents use consequences to help change their children's behaviors. **Consequences can be defined as events that follow a behavior and affect whether that behavior happens again.** They can happen naturally or they can be "applied." An example of a natural consequence is the sunburn you get when you stay out in the sun too long. An example of an applied consequence is giving some form of correction when your child misbehaves.

There are two types of consequences – positive and negative. Positive consequences, such as spending time with your child, reading together, or playing, tend to *increase* any behavior they follow. Positive consequences are things children want, and children usually are willing to do what is expected to get them.

Negative consequences tend to *decrease* any behavior they follow. Examples of negative consequences are Time-Out or loss of privileges. Children usually are willing to do what is expected to avoid negative consequences.

When your teaching includes using consequences, you help your children learn what happens as a result of their behaviors.

Using Consequences

Consequences are most effective and meaningful to your children when they meet the following requirements:

A consequence should be important to the child.

Children show us each day what is important to them. For example, if a child asks to have the same story read nearly every day, you know that reading that story is important to the child, and the storybook can be used effectively as a consequence. Pay close attention to your child's likes and dislikes because they change as children get older.

A consequence should be immediate.

Consequences that happen right after a behavior are most effective. Immediately taking a toy truck away from two brothers who are fighting over it is a more effective consequence than threatening to take the toy away and then not doing it.

A consequence should be appropriate in size.

The size of the consequence should "fit" the size of the child's behavior. A good rule is to start with the smallest consequence that you think will change the behavior. For example, if your child cleans his room, he might earn a special sweet snack like a cupcake. But you wouldn't let him have eight cupcakes for cleaning his room.

A consequence should relate to your child's behavior.

A consequence should be tied to the behavior that earned the consequence. If you use this type of consequence, children learn that their behaviors affect what happens to them in the future. For example, if two children are arguing over a toy, you might take the toy away from both of them and let them know that when they can play nicely together, they can have the toy back.

> "Parents who are afraid to put their foot down usually have children who step on their toes."
>
> – Chinese proverb

A consequence should be appropriate to your child's development level.

Make sure you choose a consequence that your child can understand. A 2-year-old won't understand a lengthy Time-Out, for example.

Categories of Consequences

Using the same consequences repeatedly with young children may eventually make the consequence ineffective. It is a good idea to vary the consequences you give, but still consistently use them in response to positive and negative behaviors. Here are some of the categories of consequences available to you as a parent. Remember to use the smallest consequence necessary to change a behavior.

Positive Consequence Categories

Activities: Fun things kids like to do, such as watching DVDs, helping bake cookies, running through the sprinkler, playing board games, being read stories, etc.

Possessions: A child's possessions are very important. A special toy, bicycle, or article of clothing could be turned into a motivator to encourage positive behaviors.

Special Foods or Snacks: Special foods are the "fun foods" that we all like to eat between meals. They can be treats like fruits, nuts, cookies, ice cream, candy, veggies, salty snacks, etc. Another way to use foods as a consequence is to allow a child to choose what to have for dinner (within reason, of course!), or to let the child prepare part of the family meal, choose next week's breakfast cereal at the store, etc.

People and Attention: Children love to spend time with the people who care for them. Spending one-on-one time with your child, even just a few minutes, can make a big difference in his or her behavior. Use hugs, smiles, pats on the back, and high-fives. Charts and stickers are another way of giving positive attention to children for their good behavior.

> "You can learn many things from children. How much patience you have, for instance."
>
> — *Franklin P. Jones*

We can't emphasize enough the importance of giving your attention to your child. Your time together need not involve elaborate plans or activities. And it need not cost money. One woman we know fondly remembers going to the airport with her father to watch planes take off and land. You can lie on your back and look at the clouds to see what kinds of pictures you can find. You can sit on the back porch on a rainy afternoon and color. You can visit a public library and read some books together. Studies show that kids will own literally hundreds of toys during their childhood, but none of those toys will mean as much as time spent with a parent.

Negative Consequence Categories

Redo/Overlearn: Having your child appropriately repeat an action or statement he or she has just done incorrectly. For instance, if your daughter is running in the house, have her walk back through the room she has run through. You might refer to the repetition as "practice," saying something like *"Now, let's practice how to walk the right way in the house."*

Redirect: Using gentle physical guidance or verbal instruction to change a young child's point of interest. In other words, a parent redirects a child toward appropriate behavior and away from inappropriate behavior. If your daughter was playing with some of your CDs, you would redirect her to the toy box, where the two of you could find a toy to play with.

Undo: Having your child appropriately undo some behavior he or she has done wrong. A good example is when a child colors on the wall. Having the child help you clean the wall is a way to "undo" the bad behavior.

Time-Out: Removing a child from the fun things in life for a short period of time. Time-Out is a very effective discipline tool because children can't participate or receive attention or reinforcement for the duration of the Time-Out. (For more information about Time-Out, see Chapter 10.)

Remove a Possession or Activity: Removing an object from the child and placing it in Time-Out for a short period of time, or taking away an opportunity to participate in something the child wants to do. An example of removing a possession would be taking a toy away from two children who are fighting over it and placing the toy in Time-Out for several minutes. An example of removing an activity would be withdrawing permission for a child to go to the park following her inappropriate behavior.

Ignore: Another way to deal with negative behaviors is to simply ignore them. But use ignoring only if you can safely let the child's behavior continue until he or she stops. As soon as the child makes any attempt toward positive behaviors, quickly focus attention on the positive behavior by praising the child.

Putting It All Together

Here's an easy formula to follow when using consequences with your children.

1. Was your child's behavior positive or negative?

2. If the behavior was positive, the child earns a positive consequence. If the behavior was negative, the child earns a negative consequence.

3. Determine how you can make a connection between the behavior and the consequence so the child can learn from the experience. For example, if the child's behavior involved not following

instructions, then choose a consequence that requires your child to follow a set of instructions. Or if your child's behavior involved squabbling with his sister, pick a consequence where he has to work cooperatively with her.

4. Choose a category of **positive** consequences that will motivate your child. A fun activity, such as helping bake cookies, might be a positive consequence for one child, but another child might prefer reading a story.

5. Choose a category of **negative** consequences that is meaningful to your child. You might want to use redirection to steer a young child away from a negative behavior, but you may choose Time-Out as a negative consequence for an older child. Because you know your child's personality, you'll be able to choose the category that is most motivating for him or her.

Helpful Hints

When giving a consequence, remember the following:

Be clear.

Make sure your child knows what the consequence is and what he or she did to earn it.

Follow through.

If your child does something to earn a positive consequence, be sure you give it to him or her. Likewise, if you give a negative consequence, don't let your child talk you out of it. If you later feel that the consequence you gave was unreasonable or given out of anger, apologize and adjust the consequence accordingly.

Use a variety of consequences.

If you use the same consequence all the time, it will gradually lose its effectiveness. Try to use a variety of consequences and tie them to the behavior you are trying to reinforce or reduce.

A 2-year-old is unable to understand the concept of an accident. No matter how you try to explain it, he will see the situation as something that was done on purpose.

Don't lecture.

Briefer is better; young children have short attention spans and will either stop listening or not understand what you are saying if you go on and on.

Avoid warnings.

Warnings mean you are merely threatening to give consequences. For example, if you tell children, *"The next time you two argue, you're both going to Time-Out,"* you're telling them what you'll do the **next time** they argue. When you warn or threaten to give consequences, you and your consequences lose effectiveness. Instead of warning, give a consequence right away. Then your kids will know that you mean what you say.

Watch your behavior when you give the consequence.

Be pleasant and enthusiastic when giving positive consequences. Be calm and matter-of-fact when giving negative consequences. Yelling and screaming are not effective when giving negative consequences. Kids won't hear your words if they can only hear your anger.

Summing Up

Consequences are the part of teaching that really helps change children's behaviors. Positive consequences increase the chances that a behavior will occur again. Negative consequences decrease the chances that a behavior will happen in the future.

Keep these ideas in mind when you choose a consequence and explain it to your child: The consequence should be important to the child, be given immediately, and be appropriate in size for the behavior and for your child's developmental level. A good rule is to start with the smallest consequence you think will change the behavior. These are the keys to using consequences that are effective.

Frequently Asked Questions
about
Giving Consequences

 "What kind of consequences can I give my 2-year-old? Is she too young to receive discipline?"

 No, 2-year-olds are not too young, but the type of discipline you use depends upon a child's age and ability. The two most frequently used consequences for children this young are giving attention for positive behavior and using redirection for misbehavior. Sometimes, you can also have your child redo a behavior, undo a behavior, or do the correct behavior more often. Don't expect immediate or long-lasting results right away; learning takes time. Be consistent, firm, and fair. Make sure your child sees that positive behavior results in a positive response from you.

 "When my child is having a tantrum it is hard to give him a consequence. What should I do?"

 Giving a child a consequence when he is out of control is probably not beneficial to you or to him. Wait until you are both calm. Then, you will be able to teach him and he will be able to learn. Read Chapters 9, 11, and 13 on Preventive Teaching, *Corrective Teaching*, and *Teaching Self-Control*. The information there is designed to help you deal with negative behaviors that lead up to or result in a temper tantrum.

"Consequences don't seem to affect my child. She seems to like getting my attention by doing bad things. What's the best way to handle this situation?"

 Kids sometimes will seek any kind of attention, positive or negative. If you give a lot of attention to misbehavior and none for positive behavior, your child will probably misbehave because that's what gets your attention. Remember to praise more than correct. Keep the attention you give to negative behavior to a minimum and increase the amount of attention your daughter receives for doing positive behaviors. That can make it more likely that she will do those positive behaviors again.

 "Sometimes I get so upset that I give my child a consequence that is way too big. I try to stay calm, but what can I do when this happens?"

 If you are too upset, take a break. A minute or two may be all you need. Take a few deep breaths and get yourself calmed down. Once you're calm, then give your child a consequence. Remember to try to deal with the problem when it is small and manageable. Also, think of consequences beforehand and stick to those so that you don't give unreasonable consequences in the "heat of battle."

"I feel like a wimp because I have a hard time giving my child a consequence. How can I get better at giving consequences?"

 Plan ahead by deciding what type of consequence you will use for certain misbehaviors, then consistently use that consequence each time those misbehaviors occur. You could even write them down and stick them on the refrigerator as a reminder to you and your child. Once you're consistently following through on giving consequences for those behaviors, you can work on changing other behaviors.

Tell Them Why

Giving Reasons Kids Understand

* *

Why won't my children do what I want them to do more often?

Why don't my children understand that their behavior affects others?

Why doesn't my child seem to know the benefits of doings things the right way?

As the parent of a young child, you have probably asked yourself these questions and others like them.

The reason young children do the things they do is because they are just that – young children. Young children have not developed the ability to think things through, understand cause and effect, or quickly learn from past mistakes. They are naturally self-centered and socially inexperienced. Many of the lessons they learn take a lot of trial and error. That's the bad news.

The good news is that there is something you can do that will help your children learn and make good choices. Look again at the list of questions. They all start with the word "why."

Giving reasons is the key to helping children understand what we are teaching them. Young children want and need to know why. They need to understand why things do and do not happen. They need to know how their behavior affects them and others. They need to know why some choices are better than others. Learning these connections helps children understand why they should be doing some things and why they shouldn't be doing other things. To help children understand these "whys," parents must give reasons.

What Are Reasons?

Reasons are statements that show children the relationship between their behavior and what could happen as a result of their behavior.

In a sense, reasons serve much the same purpose as consequences. However, there is a difference between reasons and consequences. Consequences are things that you make happen; you give something positive or negative because of what your child has done. Reasons, on the other hand, are simply statements that explain to children what might happen after they do something.

To help you better understand the difference between reasons and consequences, look at the following example of what a parent might say to a child about sharing a toy with a playmate:

Using a Consequence: *"Thank you for sharing your toy. For sharing, you can stay outside and play together for 15 more minutes."*

Giving a Reason: *"Thank you for sharing your toy. When you share with others, they are more likely to share with you."*

See the difference? Consequences are things we give or allow our children to do, while reasons are just words that explain potential outcomes.

Why Use Reasons?

So why spend all of this time on reasons? Because reasons are tools that help your teaching be more effective. Reasons also connect a child's behavior to the outcome or result of that behavior.

Research shows that children appreciate it when their parents use reasons. Reasons may help your children remember what you have taught and may make it more likely that they will actually do what you expect. Also, studies show that parents who use reasons with their children tend to be more effective.

Even very young children can understand reasons. Researchers say that reasons can be effective with children as young as 3, so use them regularly. They are powerful and important teaching tools.

> A 2-year-old's brain consumes 225% more metabolic energy than an adult's brain. That means the child is processing information at a much greater rate than the grown-up.

Types of Reasons

There are many different types of reasons you can use with your children. The most common types are reasons that show benefits, reasons that show possible negative outcomes, and reasons that teach concern for others.

In order for reasons to be effective with young children, you must use reasons that are important to them. We call these "kid reasons."

Kid reasons show your children how their behavior and decisions may affect them in the future. Keep this in mind as we look at the following types of reasons.

Benefits: "Benefit" reasons let children know the good things that could possibly happen to them when they do a positive behavior. Here are some examples of reasons that show benefits:

"When you share with others, they are more likely to share with you."

"Doing things right away helps you get back to play-time sooner."

"When you tell the truth, I'm more likely to believe you in the future."

"By putting your toys away, you'll be able to find them easier."

"The more quickly you calm down, the sooner your Time-Out will end."

Benefit reasons are the most effective type of reason to use with young children. This is because they live in a "me" world, and their first consideration in most situations is how events affect them. Benefit reasons motivate young children to do the things they should do.

Negative Outcomes: Reasons also can be used to show children how some behaviors they do may make their life more difficult. Giving "negative outcome" reasons ahead of time may help encourage children to avoid problem behaviors.

Here are some examples of negative outcome reasons:

"The dog may bite you when you are rough with him."

"You could fall and get hurt by playing on the stairs."

"When you leave toys out, they may get lost or broken."

"Others may not want to play with you when you call them names."

"When you argue about going to bed, I may not feel like reading you a story first."

Don't use negative outcome reasons to threaten or scare children into doing what you want. Instead, use these reasons to help your children learn that doing inappropriate behaviors will probably make things worse for them instead of better.

Be aware that if you rely on negative outcome reasons all the time, your kids will tend to view you as nagging and quickly tune you out.

Concern for Others: Although young children are very self-centered, we don't necessarily want them to stay that way. Children need to learn that their actions and decisions affect not only them, but others as well.

Learning this helps children understand concepts such as kindness, caring, concern, helpfulness, sorrow, empathy, and fairness. These qualities help children get along with others. Reasons that show concern for others can help children understand how their behavior affects those around them.

The following examples are reasons that can help children learn to show concern for others:

"Calling names can make others feel sad."

"Putting your shoes away makes it easier for me to vacuum the floor."

"Telling others 'Thank you' makes them feel good for helping you."

> The average 4-year-old asks more than 400 questions every day. [1]

"Hitting could hurt someone and make him cry."

"Letting someone else have a turn can make her feel special and lets her have fun."

Reasons that show concern for others are wonderful tools for beginning to teach children that they should consider others when they make choices.

When to Use Reasons

So far, you have learned what reasons are and why they are important to use with young children. Now, let's look at when we should use reasons with our young children. Typically, reasons are given to children in three types of situations: teaching, giving instructions, and telling children *"No."*

Teaching Children: Parenting a young child requires a lot of teaching and explanation. Often, our children have difficulty understanding what we expect of them and why. Reasons can be used to help children know why they should or shouldn't do certain behaviors.

> "It is a wise father that knows his own child."
>
> – *William Shakespeare*

For example, when a child does something well, a parent could use a kid reason to help that child understand why that behavior was a good thing to do. In the next chapter, you will learn how to combine praise with reasons when your children do things well. We call this *Effective Praise*.

You also can use a kid reason to help a child understand why some behaviors are not appropriate.

In Chapter 11, you will learn how to use a skill called *Corrective Teaching* to respond to your children's problem behaviors. Kid reasons work very well when teaching children how to correct problem behaviors.

Another time to use reasons is when you teach children what you expect them to do in future situations. Letting children know what you expect and why makes it more likely that they will do what you want. In Chapter 9, you will learn more about how to do this using a parenting skill called *Preventive Teaching*.

Giving Instructions to Children: It is not unusual for young children to refuse or resist when they are asked to do things. This can occur when they are asked to pick up their toys, come to dinner, go to bed, share with others, be quiet when someone is on the telephone, or go to Time-Out right away. Children are not born knowing why it is important for them to do certain tasks. If you notice a pattern where your children question your instructions or just won't do what you ask, you may want to begin using some kid reasons (especially those that show benefits) to help them understand.

Telling Children *"No"*: One of the most difficult situations for a young child is to hear the word *"No."* As adults, we understand that there are times when eating candy, going outside to play, or staying up late are not appropriate. However, youngsters struggle with the fact that they can't always have or do what they want, when they want it. Letting children know why we are saying *"No"* may help them understand the situation better and may make it easier for them to accept our decisions. Of course, with young children there are no guarantees that these situations will go smoothly every time. Still, we encourage you to try using kid reasons when telling your children *"No"* and see what happens. Over time, you may start seeing some good results.

Although these three types of situations are perfect for using kid reasons, remember that you can use a reason anytime your child needs help understanding why something should or shouldn't happen.

HeLpfuL Hints

Here are a few final thoughts on using reasons with your children:

Use kid reasons.

There are many types of reasons that can be used with children. Reasons can show what is important to parents, teachers, playmates, and others. However, the reasons that seem to work best with young children are those that are important to them. So, whenever possible, use reasons that will show your children how their behavior affects them.

Use reasons often.

We know that it can take a lot of teaching and practice before young children learn what we want them to know. This is true of learning to tie shoelaces, button a shirt, zip up a jacket, and many other things. It is also true of reasons. You may need to use a reason several times in similar situations before your child begins to understand. Over time, though, your persistence and patience will help your children learn how their behavior affects what happens to them.

Be brief.

As we've mentioned before, the attention span of young children can be very short, so the reasons you use need to be just as short.

Be real.

Even though children are young, they learn very quickly what is likely to happen and what is not. Make sure you use reasons that point out realistic outcomes of their behavior. For example, when a child makes faces at someone, warning him that his face could freeze that way probably isn't as good a reason as explaining that others may want to play with him more when he doesn't make faces at

> A 24- to 44-pound child needs five cups of water a day.

them. Reasons also need to show outcomes that will occur in the near future. For example, telling a child that picking up her toys is a sign of being responsible and that will help her get a good job someday is probably not as good a reason as telling her that her toys will be easier to find the next time.

Focus on the positive.

While it is true that unpleasant things can result when children misbehave, we don't want kids to be motivated by the fear of bad things happening. Rather, we want them to be motivated by the positive things that result from doing things well. So, limit how often you use reasons like *"You'll get hurt"* or *"You'll get into trouble."* Instead, use reasons that show your children how they, and others, can benefit from doing something well. Use reasons like *"If you put your toys away, you'll be able to find them when you want to play again"* or *"If you share, others will want to share with you."*

Summing Up

Reasons are wonderful tools to use with children, even young children. Reasons teach children how the world works by showing them what is likely to happen as a result of their behavior. These are important lessons for children to learn.

Although children understand reasons better as they get older, there is evidence that reasons are effective with children as young as 3 years old. So get in the habit of giving reasons when you teach. Both you and your children will benefit.

---

[1] Thompson, C.E. (1992). *101 Wacky facts about kids.* New York: Scholastic, Inc., Parachute Press.

Frequently Asked Questions
about
Giving Reasons

 "What is the difference between kid reasons and giving choices?"

 Kid reasons are positive statements by parents that describe what may or may not happen in the future as the result of a behavior. An example could be telling your son that picking up his toys when you ask will give him more time to play later. Choices are decisions you allow children to make in order to become more responsible and independent. An example could be having your child choose which outfit to wear. Usually, giving young children the choice between two things is enough. Too many choices can cause confusion and set up power struggles when it comes to getting your child to follow a set routine.

 "My daughter always wants a reason why she must do what I ask her to do. Does she need to have a reason to do everything?"

 No. But remember that it's developmentally normal for young children to ask why. Giving reasons helps your kids see the connection between positive behavior and positive results, and negative behavior and negative results. Be sure to focus your reasons on positive outcomes. This is a good tool for parents because children are more motivated by the positive things that may occur than by negative threats or demands. Children are more likely to follow through with a behavior when they know how it will benefit them.

Q **"When I tell my son why we are doing or not doing something, he keeps asking about it. How many reasons are enough for him?"**

A Give your child one brief, specific kid reason. If he continues to ask you about it, there are a number of things you can do. Sometimes, have your child repeat the reason back to you to see if he understands. If he repeats it, you can say, "Good job of listening to what I said." If he doesn't understand, rephrase your reason so he does understand. If you feel that he's just trying to get your attention, use redirection to get his attention on something else.

Q **"Can I use kid reasons whenever my child misbehaves?"**

A If you do, keep them brief and to the point. Remember, reasons are only part of your teaching and they don't change behavior by themselves; you also have to use consequences. Kid reasons should be positive and important to the child. Don't give reasons when you are angry. They often turn into threats.

"How is a reason different from a consequence?"

 A reason is something that may or may not happen in the future as a result of a behavior. A consequence is something that is earned and that is going to occur now as a result of a behavior.

 "At what age should I start giving reasons? At what age can I start helping my child generate his or her own reasons?"

 Start giving reasons as soon as you can. Your kids will be more likely to begin understanding them sooner, and it's a good habit for all parents to develop. Your kids may not completely understand every reason, but they will start seeing the connection between their behaviors and the results that follow.

Way to Go!

Using Praise Effectively and Often

● ●

We've stressed the importance of being good teachers for our children. There are many important teaching tools you can use to help your kids learn the life skills they need. We've already talked about some of them – understanding how children develop, nurturing, clear communication, using *Show and Tell*, selecting appropriate consequences, and giving reasons.

To this toolbox of skills let's add another essential tool – praise. Praise is one of the most powerful teaching methods you can use. Praise is like a compass. A compass is an instrument that lets us know where we are going. It's used to keep us going in the right direction. Praise works in much the same way. Praise lets children know they are heading in the right direction. Regularly using praise makes it easier for kids to stay on the right path and gets them back on track when they get lost.

If praise is so powerful, why don't parents use it as often as they should? There are several reasons. One is that it's human nature to focus on things that go wrong rather than things that go right. The cup of milk spilled on the kitchen floor requires us to wipe it up, but the cup of milk the toddler drank without spilling doesn't require our attention nearly as much.

> "Children always turn to the light."
>
> – David Hare

Another reason we may not use praise is because we don't recognize appropriate, expected behaviors as anything special. If we've already told our kids what behaviors we like, why do we have to keep telling them?

Regardless of why parents don't use praise often enough, using praise actually can make life easier. When we show our approval of what our kids are doing, they're more likely to continue to do more of the things we want them to do and fewer of the things we don't want them to do. In this chapter, we'll talk about some of the ways we can use praise to help our kids be successful and make things easier for us as parents.

We have a brief, simple, effective parenting skill for praising children. This skill is called *Effective Praise.*

Effective Praise is **responding to your children sincerely and enthusiastically for the positive behaviors they do.**

There are four steps to *Effective Praise*. They are:

1. Show approval.
2. Show and Tell the positive behavior.
3. Give a reason.
4. Give a positive consequence.

(These steps will be explained in detail later in this chapter.)

Catching your children in the act of being good and praising their behaviors is one of the easiest and most effective ways to encourage your kids to behave well in the future. Let's look at the best times to use *Effective Praise*.

When to Use Effective Praise

As a parent, you already know how busy young children can be. Yes, they can be a joy to be around, but they can also try your patience. Their natural curiosity and high energy level can lead to some very stressful days. Some days it can seem like all we do is move from one problem to another. The good things our children do easily can get lost. When this happens, we have to make a greater effort to recognize the good behavior. Generally, there are three types of situations when you can use *Effective Praise*:

When children continue to do things they already do well.

All children do some things well, even though there are days when it may seem these successes are few and far between. However, if you really look for good behavior, you can easily find it. At Boys Town, we encourage parents to watch their children and "catch 'em being good." In other words, praise the positive behaviors you see your children doing willfully. Those successes include any behaviors your children do that you would like them to do more in the future.

Successes can include your children's big accomplishments, including developmental milestones like fastening buttons, tying shoelaces, riding a tricycle, or using the potty. But successes also can include day-to-day behaviors like coming when called, sitting quietly, saying *"Please"* and *"Thank you,"* or sharing with a playmate. Remember, some children will do more of what you like if you just tell them what you like.

When children show improvements in problem behaviors.

Young children are learning and growing all of the time. They move from sitting to standing to walking in a relatively short period of time. Although we notice these milestones, it is easy to miss the steps that occur in between. The same can be true in other areas as children learn other behaviors like accepting *"No"* answers, picking up toys, or going to bed without having a tantrum. We must remember it takes some time for most of the expectations we have for our children to become a reality. Yet, every step they take in the right direction is still a right step. *Effective Praise* can be used for even the small positive steps so that they can serve as building blocks for the next step.

> "Silence is golden – unless you have a toddler. In that case, silence is very, very suspicious."
>
> — *Anonymous*

When children make positive attempts at using a new skill.

Most of the time, young children will not do things correctly the first time they try. Much of what we expect of them is either new or somewhat difficult for them. Not only will it take time for children to become skilled in some areas, but there also can be numerous mistakes, forgetfulness, and frustration along the way.

However, it is important to realize that it is a success anytime our children try to do something well, regardless of the outcome. It is a lot like trying to teach a child to hit a baseball; you have to teach the proper grip, stance, and timing. There will be many swings and misses before the child actually hits the ball. Oftentimes, children do not need our encouragement when they make contact; hitting the ball is exciting and motivating all by itself. But it is just as valuable to offer encouragement and support for trying each time the child swings and misses.

Praising children for things they attempt to learn also may provide them with the motivation to keep trying when tasks are difficult and when success doesn't come easily. Watch carefully for these situations at home, such as when your child tries to feed the dog but spills the dog food on the floor, or tries to button a shirt but misses a button. Wanting to learn and try positive behaviors are always good things, even though they may sometimes be a little messy.

What are some things your child does that you could praise? Take a few minutes to think about some things your child already does well, improvements he or she has made in skills, and attempts he or she has made to learn new things. It may help to make a list and post it on the refrigerator. Kids like to see their progress. And it's a good reminder for you to see the positive things your child does.

Steps of Effective Praise

As we mentioned earlier, *Effective Praise* is a brief, effective way to positively respond to what your child does well and to encourage him or her to do well in the future. Let's take a look at the steps of the skill.

1. Show approval.

Showing approval means immediately showing your children that you like what they did or tried to do. This can be done by using words like *"Wow," "Super," "Wonderful,"* or *"That's great!"* Approval also can be demonstrated by your actions. Smiles, hugs, kisses, and high-fives are some ways of showing approval. The goal is simply to sincerely show your kids that you approve of what they have done in a way that will encourage them to do that behavior more in the future.

2. Show and Tell the positive behavior.

To make your praise most effective, it is important to show and tell your children what they did well. Although you might assume that kids should know what you like or what they did well, it isn't that simple. Young children are often unaware of what they are doing. In fact, they often do something positive without knowing it, almost by accident. Never assume that your children know what behaviors you like them to do. You need to make sure they know. Showing and telling children what they did well makes it more likely they will do these behaviors again in the future. Examples of this step would be saying, *"You came quickly when Daddy called you!"* or *"You rode the tricycle all by yourself!"*

3. Give a reason.

Reasons are wonderful tools to use with children. Reasons teach children what is likely to happen when they use certain behaviors. A reason should be age-appropriate, relate to the child, and be realistic, brief, and positive. Kids reasons may encourage a child to do a behavior more in the future.

4. Give a positive consequence.

On most occasions, your praise and attention will be enough to encourage your children to continue to do certain positive behaviors. However, there may be some positive behaviors that are especially difficult for them to master or ones that occur on rare occasions.

For these behaviors, which might include accomplishments like mastering potty training or learning to ride a tricycle, it may be necessary to add a little "oomph" to your praise. This can easily be done by rewarding your child with a positive consequence.

Positive consequences are things your child likes that reinforce the behavior you want. Positive consequences may range from smiles, pats, and hugs to more tangible things like special time with a parent, privileges, and possessions. For a refresher on using consequences effectively, look back at Chapter 5. Keep in mind, though, that most of the time and for most behaviors, your praise and approval will be enough.

Using Effective Praise

Effective Praise not only can benefit you and your child, but also can be done quickly and easily. Read the following examples and see how easy it can be.

Example 1

1. Show approval.
- Give a praise statement.
- Smile, hug, and touch.

"Wow! Good job!"

2. Show and Tell the positive behavior.
- Specifically describe or demonstrate the skill or behavior.

"You picked up your toys right away!"

3. Give a reason.
- Make it developmentally appropriate.
- Be brief.

"Since you picked up your toys, you now have time to do something fun."

4. Give a positive consequence.
- Contingent on behavior.
- Appropriate for the situation.

"Let's read your favorite story."

Example 2 ....

1. **Show approval.**

   "Don't worry about the little spill. I'm proud of you for trying!"

2. **Show and Tell the positive behavior.**

   "You're starting to learn to pour your own glass of juice."

3. **Give a reason.**

   "Pretty soon, you may be able to get your own juice."

4. **Give a positive consequence.**

   "You're getting to be such a big girl. Here, you take this towel and wipe up the spill and I'll help you finish pouring."

Example 3 ....

1. **Show approval.**

   "That was much better!"

2. **Show and Tell the positive behavior.**

   "Look, you have the first three buttons fastened."

3. **Give a reason.**

"Just think, you aren't going to need Mom's help to get dressed soon."

4. **Give a positive consequence.**

"You're getting more buttoned each time." (Give child a hug.)

As you read through these examples, you can see that *Effective Praise* is an easy way to respond when children are successful, show improvements, and make attempts to do things well. In the future, try using *Effective Praise* often with your child. Notice your child's reaction and be aware of how you improve in recognizing behavior to praise.

Before we close the chapter, there are just a few things to remember about making your praise most effective.

Helpful Hints

Here are a few suggestions for how best to use *Effective Praise.*

Be sincere and enthusiastic.

You want to truly celebrate your children's successes, improvements, and positive attempts. If your children see that you are excited about good behaviors, they also may get excited about doing well. With your approval, you are showing your children that doing well is more exciting than being disobedient. Again, this doesn't mean that you must literally jump for joy every time your kids do well. It does mean that your children should easily be able to tell you are pleased and that your praise is real and heart-felt. Let your approval show.

Be brief and specific.

We know that young children have very short attention spans. The great thing about *Effective Praise* is that it does not take very long to do. A good rule to follow is that your praise should not take longer than the behavior you are praising. Also, as you praise your children, remember to clearly show and tell them what they did well. When children know what they did well, it makes it easier for them to repeat that behavior in the future.

Focus on the positive.

One of the goals of *Effective Praise* is to increase the frequency of positive behaviors. For this to occur, make sure you are praising children for doing something well rather than for not doing something naughty. For example, instead of saying something like *"Thank you for not arguing and complaining,"* you should say *"Thank you for saying 'Okay' and picking up your toys right away."*

Praise the "do well" behaviors rather than the absence of "bad" behavior.

Praise more than you correct.

As young children are learning and exploring, they will certainly provide plenty of opportunities for parents to respond to problem behaviors. Even though you must deal with these situations, you do not want to be constantly correcting your children. We want to enjoy our children and have them enjoy being around us.

To avoid feeling like you are merely moving from one problem to another, look carefully for good things that happen in the middle of difficult situations. For example, when correcting a child for hitting a sibling, there may be an opportunity to praise behaviors such as stopping the hitting, coming to you when called, looking at you and listening while you are talking, accepting a consequence, and making an apology.

In addition, there may be opportunities right after the correction to praise behaviors like sharing and getting along with others. Even though you must correct problem behaviors, giving praise frequently lets your children

> "Nothing improves a child's hearing more than a few kind words."

know that they are more likely to hear good things than bad things when they are around you.

Summing Up

Some parents tell us that even though they praise their children, it just doesn't seem to make any difference in their kids' behavior. Usually, we find that these parents praise only the outstanding achievements or momentous occasions. They are missing many everyday opportunities to focus on positive behaviors, the little things that kids do all the time. After these parents begin looking closely for small improvements and praising them, they notice many positive changes in their kids' behavior. In addition, the parents feel they get along better with their kids. This is not coincidence. Praise works.

Other parents have asked us, *"Why should I praise my kids for something they're supposed to do?"* Good question. We answer them with these questions: *"Do you like being recognized for the things you do well, regardless of whether you're supposed to do them? Do you like to hear your boss tell you what a good job you're doing?"* Most parents say *"Of course."* And then add, *"And, I wouldn't mind hearing it a little more often."* Enough said. We all like to hear about things we do well.

Additionally, we have had parents tell us that they praise their children often, but it doesn't seem to mean much to them. The problem is that these parents tend to praise their kids for everything! Their praise is not contingent on their kids' positive behavior. It's no different than giving kids ice cream every time they turn around. Sooner or later, no matter how much a kid likes ice cream, it's going to lose its attractiveness. Praise also loses its impact if it is dished up without being tied to a specific behavior.

Effective Praise is supposed to be both frequent and tied to positive behavior. That's why it works! Parents provide praise and encouragement for very specific things their kids have done. This attention to specific behavior increases the likelihood that the same behaviors will occur again.

Your children give you something to be happy about. All kids do something that deserves praise. Make sure you recognize it, and most of all, tell them.

One final note: In interviews with some of the thousands of people who have completed our parenting program, many have consistently told us that *Effective Praise* has had a lasting impact on their families. Parents find themselves being more positive about their kids. Kids, in turn, are more positive about their parents. With *Effective Praise*, everybody wins.

Frequently Asked Questions
about
Effective Praise

 "Am I supposed to give my child something every time she does something right?"

 Not necessarily. Both praise and positive consequences can be used frequently at first to increase the things she doesn't do routinely. Later, for things your child does regularly, a word of encouragement and a positive touch, a smile, a wink, or eye contact can be powerful enough.

 "Isn't praise just like a bribe?"

 No. We have learned how important it is to reward good behavior so that it will continue to happen. Praise is earned after good behavior. It is not a bribe but a way of showing your appreciation and approval to your children for a positive behavior they did. A bribe is actually given after bad behavior in the hopes that the misbehavior will stop or that good behavior will occur. An example would be, *"If you stop crying, I'll buy you a candy bar."* Bribes don't work because you're only encouraging negative behavior to occur again.

"Why should I praise my child for behavior he already does well?"

 Children need to know you appreciate the things they do well. Your child will see your praise as more personal if you praise him for things he already does well and not just for things you want him to improve. As your child masters a certain behavior, you may choose to say nothing – just give a "thumbs up," a nod, or a smile to acknowledge a job well done. Don't take positive behavior for granted. If you do, you'll find yourself focusing on all of the negative things your child does.

 "My child is finally starting to eat all her food. How long am I going to have to praise her for it?"

 As we said in our previous answer, praise her until the behavior becomes a routine or habit. You may give less verbal praise, and instead give encouragement or a pat on the back as she starts to do it more often. But don't ignore it altogether.

 "I don't think my child does more good things than bad things. How am I going to praise him more often than I correct him?"

 The first key is not waiting for something outstanding to happen before you give him praise. Look closely for the little things he does well. Set up opportunities for him to succeed and then praise him for those accomplishments. Try to spend more time with your son doing fun things and watch closely for positive behaviors. It's a great habit for all parents to get into.

"I tell my child all the time when she does something right, but it doesn't seem to change anything. What should I do?"

 Be patient. Praise is sometimes like water running over a rock – over time, the persistent flow of the water changes the shape of the rock. Your child may need just a little more time to respond. Perhaps increasing your enthusiasm and showing your affection with a smile, a hug, or a pat on the back can communicate your feelings better. If you're not already doing so, occasionally give a small reward. If you are giving a reward and you think it's not working, review the chapter on consequences to see if you're following the guidelines described there.

8

Step by Step

Teaching Social Skills to Kids

* *

Children need to be taught so much – everything from how to eat, get dressed, and tie shoelaces to sharing, safety rules, and doing what they're asked. We have so much to teach them, it's hard to know where to begin.

In this chapter and the next, we'll look at two important elements of the teaching you do as a parent. This chapter will focus on what to teach kids. In the next chapter, we'll look at *Preventive Teaching*, or *how* to teach kids.

What Should I Teach?

For most parents, it's easy to identify the things we *don't want* our children to do. Yelling, arguing, hitting, complaining, and lying are just a few behaviors that come to mind. What we often don't think about are the things we want our children to do instead.

We know that just telling our children what *not* to do doesn't work. If it did, we wouldn't have to keep saying it! If we truly want our children to be successful, we must be able to clearly teach the things we want them to do.

Social Skills

There are many things parents need to teach their children to do for themselves. Examples include doing tasks, following routines, caring for themselves, etc. Yet, one of the most overlooked areas has to do with teaching children how to interact with others.

And what an important part of life that is! After all, children (and adults) spend more time in social situations than they do tying shoelaces, getting dressed, or putting away items. Since it is so important for children to know how to do this successfully, social skills are a necessity.

Social skills are sets of behaviors that allow our children to get along with others effectively and pleasantly, both at home and away from home. We sometimes refer to these as "civilizing" skills. Some examples of social skills are *Following Instructions, Listening to Others, Asking Permission, Waiting Your Turn, Accepting "No" Answers,* and *Sharing.*

To identify what skills you would like your child to learn, take a piece of paper and write down two skills that you want your child to do *more consistently,* such as doing what you ask or not arguing when the answer is *"No."* Remember to choose skills that your child is capable of learning and doing, and that fit your child's age and developmental level.

Also, write down two *new* skills your child needs to learn, such as waiting for his turn or saying she's sorry.

Next, take one of the skills you have identified and ask yourself this question: *"If I ask my child to do this skill, what do I want him or her to say and do?"*

Starting Out

Since each social skill is a set of behaviors, teaching the skills is a gradual process. It begins by showing and telling a behavior or two of the skill you want your child to learn. For very young children, the first step may be simply to look at you when you speak. As that behavior improves, you can add another step, such as having your child say *"Okay"* or nod his or her head when you give an instruction. As your child's ability to demonstrate these two behaviors together improves, you can add more steps. Eventually, your child will learn all the steps that make up the skill you want to teach. On the next page are some behaviors that make up many social skills. (In the chart on page 125 are some common social skills parents can teach young children who are able to do these individual behaviors.)

* Look at the person.
* Say *"Okay."*
* Do what was asked.
* Check back.
* Sit or stand quietly.
* Find something quiet to do.
* Say *"Thank you."*
* Say *"Please"* or *"May I...."*
* Ask for what you want.
* Say *"I'm sorry."*
* Tell what you did wrong.
* Ask once and wait.

Where to Go from Here

Young children learn better when lessons are brief, consistent, and repeated often. Teaching is also more clear when it is focused on one or two topics. Thus, it will benefit you and your children if you start with just one or two social skills. One way to teach these behaviors and skills is to use *Preventive Teaching*, which we will discuss in the next chapter.

Other ways to teach your children social skills include:

* **Use *Effective Praise* each time** your child uses a social skill or shows improvement in using a social skill.

Social Skills

Following Instructions

- Look at the person.
- Say *"Okay."*
- Do what was asked.
- Check back.

Asking Permission

- Look at the person.
- Say *"Please"* or *"May I…."*
- Ask for what you want.
- Say *"Thank you."*

Accepting "No" for an Answer

- Look at the person.
- Say *"Okay."*
- Sit or stand quietly.

Getting Someone's Attention

- Look at the person.
- Sit or stand quietly.
- Ask once and wait.
- Say *"Thank you."*

Waiting Your Turn

- Sit or stand quietly.
- Find something quiet to do.
- Say *"Thank you"* when your turn is over.

Asking for Help

- Look at the person.
- Say *"Please."*
- Ask for help.
- Say *"Thank you"* when you get it.

Listening to Others

- Look at the person.
- Sit or stand quietly.
- Say *"Okay."*

Saying You're Sorry

- Look at the person.
- Say *"I'm sorry."*
- Tell what you did wrong.

✳ **Model social skills for your children.** This can be done anytime you are with them or when you interact with others as your children are watching.

✳ **Make learning fun.** For example, use *Show and Tell* to describe to your child how to listen closely when you are talking. Then use the game "Red Light, Green Light" to practice listening. The game works like this: Tell your child that he or she can walk toward you only when you say *"Green light."* If you say *"Red light,"* your child must stop walking. As your child stands facing you, alternately say *"Green light"* and *"Red light."* These games help children follow instructions and listen attentively. Offer lots of praise throughout the game. Your child will learn that listening closely to you isn't something he or she should do only when you are correcting him or her.

You can use other games to teach other skills and behaviors, such as "Mother May I?" for asking permission. You also can use other motivational techniques, such as placing stickers on charts, as a way to motivate young children to learn new behaviors. (See the chart section at the end of this chapter for more information.)

Helpful Hints

Be brief.

We can't stress this enough. Young children have short attention spans. For them to learn any lesson, it has to be simple and short.

Be consistent.

Young children rarely learn something new the first time it is taught. Social skills are no different. You may need to teach the same social skill many times before your child is able to use it. Teaching a social skill often and the same way each time can help.

Be a model.

Young children often learn and remember by watching you and others. Show them how to do the skill you are teaching by using it in everyday life. Use your child's desire to be like you to your advantage.

Practice.

Young children also learn well by doing. Give them opportunities to try saying and doing each step of the social skill you are teaching. (You will learn more about how to make practice effective and fun for young children in the next chapter.)

Using Charts to Motivate Your Child

Charts can be a great way to motivate children to learn new behaviors. Many parents enjoy coming up with creative charts for their kids. Some of the most creative designs come from kids themselves. Young children, in particular, love to get out the crayons and make a colorful chart. This is a positive way to get your child involved in the process and gives you more opportunities to praise.

> More than 30,000 sets of twins are born in the United States each year.

The charts at the end of this chapter target certain behaviors, but you can adapt them for other behaviors or create your own charts. The rewards listed on each chart are suggestions; you may want to use other rewards that your child will find motivating. Review Chapter 5 for more information about positive consequences that will help motivate your child.

Summing Up

There are so many teaching responsibilities on parents' shoulders. It is up to you to make sure your children know how to follow instructions, wait their turn, ask for help, get along with others, show respect, and be successful in school, to name just a few areas where kids must learn what to do.

The task of preparing our children for success (both now and for a lifetime) can seem overwhelming. Yet, like most difficult jobs, this one can be broken down into smaller, more manageable parts. Sure, we are responsible for teaching our children everything they need to know. But combining the idea of teaching social skills with the parenting skills you learn in this book (*Effective Praise, Preventive Teaching,* and *Corrective Teaching*) will make the job easier for you.

As you and your child begin to experience success, we are certain you will find that teaching your child social skills provides hope in your children's future and satisfaction in being their first and most important teacher. Remember, teaching our children is not merely a responsibility, it is an amazing opportunity.

Bedtime Bonanza

Weekday bedtime is 8:30 p.m.

MONDAY	TUESDAY	WEDNESDAY

THURSDAY	FRIDAY

Each night I go straight to bed and stay in bed, I get a sticker to put on my chart. In the morning, I can use my sticker to get a special morning snack. If I have at least four stickers at the end of the week, I can stay up until 9 p.m. on weekends with my parents.

Building Blocks for Better Behavior

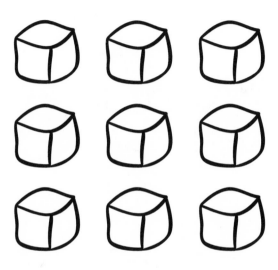

Each time my mom finds me playing nicely with my sister, I get to color in a block. When three blocks are colored, I get the reward.

Morning behavior: Playing nicely with my sister.
Reward: Mom reads me a book.

Afternoon behavior: Playing nicely with my sister.
Reward: I can watch a video.

Evening behavior: Playing nicely with my sister.
Reward: I can play catch with Dad.

Beach Ball Bonus

Each day I pick up my toys, I get to color a beach ball. Each day I color a ball, I get to play a game with Mom or Dad for 15 minutes.

End-of-the-Week Bonuses

* **Five balls colored:** Spend special time with Mom or Dad
* **Six balls colored:** Friends come over to play on Saturday
* **Seven balls colored:** Pick a special food for Sunday dinner

My Morning Stars

	Get Dressed	Make Bed	Eat Breakfast	Brush Teeth	Ready to Leave on Time
Mon.					
Tues.					
Wed.					
Thurs.					
Fri.					
Sat.					
Sun.					

* **Three stars:** a special snack, play outside 10 minutes longer, or use a special cup at dinner
* **Four or more stars:** go to bed 15 minutes later, call Grandma or Grandpa on the phone, play a game with Mom or Dad

Potty Time Calendar

	☀️ Morning	🏠 Afternoon	🌙 Evening
Mon.			
Tues.			
Wed.			
Thurs.			
Fri.			
Sat.			
Sun.			

I can earn three happy faces each day for using the potty.

* **One Happy Face:** Piggyback ride to bed
* **Two Happy Faces:** Piggyback ride and bike ride
* **Three Happy Faces:** Play the game I choose, piggyback ride, and bike ride

9

An Ounce of Prevention

Teaching Before Problems Occur

. . . .

We said earlier in this book that teaching is one of the most important responsibilities we have as parents. Without our teaching, our children would not acquire the skills they need to become successful and responsible adults. In this chapter, we'll look at ways to help you prevent problems and become more proactive teachers.

Think of all the lessons we teach our children, everything from how to use a spoon to how to be a good friend. Most everything young children learn, they learn from their parents. This includes social, academic, spiritual, independent-living, and healthy-living skills, all of which lay the groundwork for a successful life. Some examples of each are listed here:

Social skills:	Staying calm, getting along with others, making friends, sharing, listening, saying *"Please"* and *"Thank you,"* playing, etc.
Academic skills:	Reading, spelling, counting, organizing things, asking questions, asking for help, etc.
Spiritual skills:	Praying, sitting quietly during worship service, helping others, etc.
Independent-living skills:	Gathering laundry, helping around the house, cleaning up, safety skills, etc.
Healthy-living skills:	Brushing teeth, washing hands, hygiene skills, etc.

Teaching these skills is a wonderful opportunity to shape the lives of your children in happy and successful ways. In this chapter, you will learn a parenting skill that can be used to teach your children some of the vital life lessons they need to learn. This skill is called *Preventive Teaching*. *Preventive Teaching* is **teaching your children what they should do in a future situation and practicing it in advance.**

There are four steps to *Preventive Teaching.* They are:

1. Show and Tell the desired behavior.
2. Give a reason.

3. Practice.

4. Show approval.

(These steps will be explained in detail later in this chapter.)

Preventive Teaching can be used to teach your child almost anything, including the skills we mentioned earlier. The key is to use the teaching at the right time so it is most effective.

When to Use Preventive Teaching

Many parents spend most of their time reacting to their children's behavior, often focusing simply on the negative things their kids do. We're encouraging you to be proactive when you teach by anticipating what your child should say or do in a situation (especially those where negative behaviors could occur), before the situation occurs.

Keeping this in mind, *Preventive Teaching* focuses on preventing negative behaviors and teaching kids new or alternative behaviors before they need to use them. *Preventive Teaching* helps us set our children up for success, prevent problems from happening, and teach our children to make good decisions.

Remember to use *Preventive Teaching* when kids are paying attention and are not tired, cranky, or being corrected for misbehavior. Identify the skills your kids need to learn and then use *Preventive Teaching* to teach them how to successfully use these skills.

In general, there are two types of situations where *Preventive Teaching* is most helpful – **before new situations** and **before situations where your child has had difficulty in the past.**

Before new situations: Your child will soon face a new situation where he or she might not know what to do.

> "In automobile terms, the child supplies the power but the parents have to do the steering."
>
> — *Benjamin Spock*

It might be going to a new day care or preschool, having a new baby sitter, learning new routines or chores, meeting new friends, going to new places, etc. Because the situations are unfamiliar, most children won't know what is expected or appropriate. Rather than let them struggle along on their own, you can use *Preventive Teaching* to teach your children how to handle the situation successfully.

For example, if your 5-year-old daughter is going to a friend's birthday party where there will be kids she doesn't know, you could have her practice how to say *"Hi"* or how to introduce herself. Use statements that are brief, clear, and specific. You could say, *"When you don't know someone, you can walk up to her and say, 'Hi, my*

name is Kimberly.' *Then you could ask her name if she
didn't already tell you. This will help you make friends.
Okay? Why don't you pretend I'm a girl you don't know
and then tell me your name.* (Daughter does a good practice.) *Great, nice job practicing."* Then you could give
your daughter a hug for practicing so well.

As always, choose skills and behaviors to teach that
are in line with your child's age and developmental
level. While you might work on a more complex skill,
like greeting someone, with a 5-year-old, simpler skills,
like saying *"Please,"* would be more appropriate for a
younger child.

**Before situations where your child has had dif-
ficulty in the past:** Young children have short
memories and limited life experiences. This can make
it difficult for them to learn from past mistakes. They
can easily get in the habit of making the same mistakes
over and over. Unless they learn a different way of handling these situations, children are likely to continue
this pattern of poor behavior. *Preventive Teaching* can
help change this pattern.

For example, if children have a hard time accepting
"No" for an answer, *Preventive Teaching* can be used
before the next time they ask for something. If children
struggle with getting ready in the morning, *Preventive
Teaching* can be used to help them learn a new morning
routine. For children who have difficulty playing with

others, *Preventive Teaching* can be used before they go to preschool or out to play.

Preventive Teaching allows parents to be more intentional in their instruction. It gives parents a consistent way to teach children routines, expectations, and new skills, and how to make good choices. Each time you use *Preventive Teaching*, you increase your child's chances of being successful. Let's look closer at the steps of *Preventive Teaching*.

Steps of Preventive Teaching

As we said earlier, *Preventive Teaching* has four steps: **Show and Tell the desired behavior, Give a reason, Practice,** and **Show approval.** We've already talked about *Show and Tell* (in Chapter 4), giving a reason, and showing approval (both in Chapter 7 for *Effective Praise*), so we're simply adding one new step – **practice** – in this chapter.

Here's how the four steps work:

1. Show and Tell the desired behavior.

In *Preventive Teaching, Show and Tell* is used to clearly let children know what you want them to do. *Show and Tell* can be used to teach new skills, new routines, or anything else you want your child to learn. Just remember to be brief and specific. The clearer you are in your teaching, the easier it will be for your children to learn and do what you are teaching. You may need to demonstrate or help your child the first few times you teach something that is new or difficult.

> "Nothing you do for your children is ever wasted."
>
> – *Garrison Keillor*

Example: *"Molly, when you want some more fruit, just say, 'More fruit, please.'"*

2. Give a reason

Reasons teach children what is likely to happen when they use certain behaviors. A reason should be age-appropriate, relate to the child, and be realistic, brief, and positive. Kid reasons may encourage a child to do the behavior more often in the future.

Example: *"When you ask with a 'Please,' you are more likely to get the snack you want."*

3. Practice.

Think of something you are skilled at doing. It may be your job, a parenting task, driving a car, a sport or hobby, playing a musical instrument, etc. Remember when you first started doing that activity or task? Chances are, you weren't very skilled at it the first few times. In fact, it may have taken you weeks or months to master the activity or task. Yet, the more you practiced, the more skilled and confident you became. Now, you can probably do that activity or task almost without thinking about it. This is especially true if you had a knowledgeable, skilled person helping you to practice. We want our children to experience the same benefits of practicing.

Many of the things you want your children to be skilled at are new or difficult for them. From a child's perspective, staying calm, accepting *"No"* answers, following instructions, making a bed, coming when called, cleaning a bedroom, and sharing with others are difficult tasks. Yet, with some practice and your support and encouragement, your child can begin to make improvements in these areas.

Getting young children to practice and try new things is usually easy. They are often eager to please their parents and are almost always willing to learn new things. Practice is even easier when you make it fun; ways to do this include pretending, playing games, or using actual situations. Let's take a look at each of these:

* **Pretending:** Young children love to "make believe." Pretending can be an easy way to get them to try something new. Pretending that the phone is ringing so a child can practice answering, pretend-

ing your fingers are candles that your child can blow out to help him calm down, pretending that you are someone your child does not know so he can learn to stay away from strangers, or pretending it is bedtime to practice a new nighttime routine all are ways you can practice with your child.

* **Playing Games:** Young children are almost always excited to play games. Parents can use games as a fun way for children to practice new skills. Examples include using "Mother May I?" to practice asking permission, playing "Simon Says" so children can practice following instructions, making up a race-against-the-clock contest to see who can get ready for bed the fastest, or playing musical chairs to practice how to calmly accept losing or disappointment.

* **Using Actual Situations:** Using real situations is a wonderful way to have children practice. This involves teaching just prior to the actual event or helping a child through a real situation. For example, rather than just telling your children how to clean their bedrooms, you could actually work with them to show them where to put things. Another example would be teaching your child how to follow instructions just before you ask him or her to do something.

4. Show approval.

This means showing your children that you appreciate them and their efforts to learn. As we said earlier, approval can be shown through smiles, winks, touches and hugs, or positive words. It's important to let your kids know that they've practiced well and to encourage them to actually do what you have taught them. Teaching children how to be successful should be a positive experience for both parents and children. Use your approval to help your child look forward to more of your teaching in the future.

> "There was never a child so lovely but his mother was glad to get him to sleep."
>
> — *Ralph Waldo Emerson*

Example: *"Way to go! You said 'Please' when you asked for more fruit! Dad's really proud of you!"*

Now that you've read all the steps of *Preventive Teaching*, you may be thinking, "This sounds pretty good, but when am I going to find time to use it?" The answer is that *Preventive Teaching* doesn't really take very long. Read through the following example for teaching the skill of *Following Instructions* and see how quickly it can actually occur.

Example ·

1. **Show and Tell the desired behavior.**
   - Label the skill.
   - Specifically describe the skill steps or behavior.
   - Be brief.

"Hannah, when Mommy or Daddy asks you to do something, I want you to say 'Okay' and do it right away."

2. **Give a reason.**
   - Make it developmentally appropriate.
   - Be brief.

"That way it gets done and you can go back to playing."

3. **Practice.**
   - Use pretend, play, or an actual situation.
   - Have the child actually do what was taught.
   - Be brief.

"Let's pretend that I asked you to put your shoes away. Say 'Okay' and show me how fast you can do that. Ready... Set... Go!" (Child follows parent's instruction.)

4. **Show approval.**
   - Use words of praise and encouragement.
   - Include smiles, touches, hugs, etc.

"Hannah, that was super! You put your shoes away so quickly, and you even remembered to say, 'Okay. (Parent gives child a hug.) *We'll practice some more later."*

Preventive Teaching truly gives you a quick, consistent way to teach children how to be successful or make positive changes in areas that have caused problems in the past. And once your children learn the lessons you're teaching, you'll spend less time dealing with behavior problems. Use *Preventive Teaching* often to teach many different behaviors and skills. It can be a very powerful and effective method for helping your child succeed in many different situations.

Teaching Kids How to Stay Calm

Of all the skills you can teach your children using *Preventive Teaching*, staying calm might be the most important. Young children have a hard time managing their emotions or understanding the emotions of others. They haven't yet learned how to identify feelings or talk about those feelings, and they often lack the experience it takes to make good decisions. It is especially hard for young children to stay calm when they are frustrated or angry. When these emotions rise, young children may react in different ways. They can become very aggressive and hurtful, passive and quiet, or sad and tearful. These types of behaviors create situations that can be unpleasant and frustrating for both kids and parents.

When it comes to dealing with tantrums, defiance, or other out-of-control behavior, prevention is the best approach. Children who have many opportunities to learn how to control their emotions by practicing when they are calm have a better chance of knowing what to do when they get upset.

It is difficult to teach children anything when they are upset and cranky. That is why parents must consistently use *Preventive Teaching* when their children are calm and willing to listen and learn.

> "Children have more need of models than critics."
> – *Carolyn Coats*

Teaching and practicing calm-down methods during these "neutral" times allows parents to prepare their children for times when emotions might get out of hand. Then, when an emotional situation occurs, parents can model the behavior they want their children to do and remind them about how they practiced to calm down.

Some effective calming methods are simple prompts to count to five or ten, or take a deep breath. These are good techniques for parents as well. Another useful method is to have a place for your child to go when he or she becomes upset. You simply tell your child to go to the "calm-down spot." (Make sure you can monitor the child in his or her spot.) Or your child can go get a favorite toy, pillow, or blanket. Often, these objects help calm your child and provide the comfort of having an object that he or she associates with pleasant thoughts. Parents and children can practice all these techniques.

Some parents we've worked with have even created a "Calm Down Kit." They put some simple objects in a box or bowl and have their children practice getting something from it to calm down. The items ranged from old baby toys or rattles, to a fuzzy ball, family photographs, or pictures cut out of a magazine.

Putting together a plan to help kids stay calm has many other benefits for children. Working together with their parents, children develop their thinking skills by coming up with ideas for calming down. During practice, children improve their emotional skills by acting out situations that help them understand their emotions and others' emotions.

Remember that your children cannot learn and use these strategies by themselves. It is up to you to model for your children, teach and practice with them ahead of time, and help them to use these calm-down methods when they are upset.

Helpful Hints

Here are a few things to keep in mind when using *Preventive Teaching*.

Teach at a neutral time.

You cannot teach your children much unless they are paying attention to what you are saying and doing. Your teaching also won't be very effective if you are distracted by other things. *Preventive Teaching* works best when it is used at a neutral time – when parents and children are calm and not busy or distracted.

Teach before problems occur.

Using *Preventive Teaching* in the middle of a problem will probably not be effective. Children who have more opportunities to learn skills by frequently practicing ahead of time will have a better chance of knowing what to do in a wide variety of situations. Use *Preventive Teaching* to set your children up for success and maybe you'll have fewer problem behaviors to respond to later.

Teach the positive.

Teach children what they should do. Use the steps of *Preventive Teaching – Show and Tell* the positive behavior, Give a reason, Practice, Show approval – to teach your children behaviors you want them to do.

Be brief.

Remember that the more you talk, the less your children listen. Teach, practice, and encourage in brief sentences. For example: *"To calm down, take a deep breath. Now we sit down. Then ask for help."*

Teach frequently.

Young children are usually not one-trial learners. Many skills and tasks, even simple ones, are difficult for youngsters at first. It may take some time for your child to develop a skill in a certain area. Have patience and give your child the time he or she needs. For some children, and with some skills, you may have to use *Preventive Teaching* several days in a row for improvement to be noticeable. Using games, books, verbal prompts, stickers, and other little reminders can be good ways to keep your young child interested in working on the skill you want him or her to learn over time. Remember to be patient and persistent.

Use reasons.

Children are often more likely to try new things when they understand why they should. Using "kid reasons" while doing *Preventive Teaching* can help your children understand how they can benefit from doing what you are teaching them. For instance, what are some good reasons for why young children should learn to calm down that show a benefit for them? One might be, *"When you are calm, I'm more likely to listen to you."* Another reason might be, *"The sooner you get quiet and calm, the sooner you can get back to the fun things you like."*

Practice.

We already have discussed why it is important to have children practice new skills. Yet, this point cannot be emphasized enough. Children are much more likely to remember things they have actually done than things they have just been told to do. For example, when schools teach young children fire drills, they don't just tell the children what to do – they practice the drills. Young children need to know how an experience feels and go through each step of a skill until they feel comfortable with it. Practice makes it possible for children to use all of their developmental abilities to learn and remember what you have taught.

Summing Up

Parents often tell us they get tired of correcting their children. *"I sound like a broken record,"* parents say. *"It seems like I'm always saying 'Don't do this' or 'Stop that.' And you know what? I don't think my kids even hear me anymore."*

Using *Preventive Teaching* can help you toss out that broken record. When you use *Preventive Teaching*, you help your children know what to do in new situations and prepare them for situations that have been difficult in the past. In short, you're helping your kids be successful and saving yourself the frustration of issuing corrections that sometimes are ignored or ineffective.

Preventive Teaching also has another important benefit – it allows you and your child to spend time together. Taking the time to be with your children and showing them you care by teaching helps improve relationships, and that benefits the whole family.

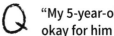

Frequently Asked Questions
about
Preventive Teaching

Q "My 5-year-old thinks practicing is a game. Is it okay for him to think we are playing?"

A At times, practicing can be a fun part of *Preventive Teaching* and it can be like playing. Children learn many lessons during play activities. If the skill you're teaching is serious, make the practice realistic (saying *"No"* to strangers). For less serious issues, have some fun practicing skills with your kids. Remember to prompt your child to use the skill you've practiced when a real situation occurs, and give a reminder about using the skill just before a situation where the skill should be used.

Q "What if I go through *Preventive Teaching* and my child still misbehaves?"

A You may need to improve how you do *Preventive Teaching* or increase the number of times you practice a skill with your child. Most children won't learn the first time they're taught something. Keep using *Preventive Teaching* and encourage the behavior you taught by using *Effective Praise* and positive consequences. If the misbehavior continues, use *Corrective Teaching* (Chapter 11).

"If my child doesn't want to practice, should I make him?"

 No. If your child resists, postpone the practice until later. But make sure you practice soon after, or your child will frequently avoid practicing. Wait for a neutral time when he is calm or wants to be with you. Use this new opportunity to practice!

 "Can I use *Preventive Teaching* to help my daughter learn what she should do in serious situations she may face?"

 Definitely. Show and tell her what she should say or do in those situations. Let her know what adults will help her and how to ask for help. As parents, we try to prepare our children for positive and negative experiences. We want them to be aware of how to react and how to prevent future serious problems. Issues such as stranger danger, playground safety, and other precautions can be effectively taught using *Preventive Teaching*.

 "When should I start using *Preventive Teaching* with my young child?"

 As soon as your child is able to understand what you are trying to teach and can follow the steps you describe.

10

Let's Take a Break!

When and How to Use Time-Out

* *

One of the most effective consequences parents can use when their young children misbehave is Time-Out. The process of Time-Out involves removing your child from the good things in life, for a small amount of time, immediately after misbehavior. It's a way of disciplining without raising your hand or voice. Time-Out is simply having your child sit quietly in one place for a certain amount of time.

Time-Out also can be defined as the opposite of what we call Time-In. Time-In is the time a young child spends doing enjoyable, fun things – playing with you, coloring, drawing, reading, watching television, playing with toys, or doing anything else he or she likes to do. Time-In is the "good stuff" in a child's life. Much of that enjoyment can come from being around you, especially when you make a point of showing affection, praising your child for good behavior, and nurturing. Time-Out is such a powerful consequence because Time-In is so important to a child.

Time-Out is a lot like the penalty used for hockey players. When a hockey player does something wrong, he is required to go to the penalty area for a certain amount of time. The referee does not scream at, threaten, or hit the player. He merely blows the whistle and points to the penalty area. During the penalty time, the player is not allowed to play, only to watch. Time-Out bothers hockey players because they would rather play than watch. Keep this hockey comparison in mind when using Time-Out with your child. Time-Out works well because children would rather be playing and doing other things they like than "sitting out."

The steps of Time-Out are simple and brief:

1. Describe the problem behavior.
2. Send or take the child to Time-Out.
3. Allow the child time to calm down.
4. Set the timer.
5. Tell the child when Time-Out is over.

Preventive Teaching for Time-Out

At a time when your child is not misbehaving, explain in simple language what Time-Out is, which problem behaviors Time-Out will be used for, and how long Time-Out will last. Practice using Time-Out with your child before using it as a consequence. You will find that several trial runs may help the real thing go better.

While practicing, remind your child you are "pretending" this time. It may be necessary to teach your children only one or two steps at a time. Teaching one or two steps instead of all of them at once may help your children clearly understand how Time-Out will work.

Try not to make the practice a chore or a lecture. Children won't listen if they think it is boring or work. A stuffed animal, doll, or action figure can be used to make the teaching more interesting. Your child can pretend the toy is a child who needs to go to Time-Out. After you have described the process to your child, help him or her show and tell you how each step goes.

When Time-Out Isn't Working

There will be times, especially when you first start using Time-Out as a consequence, when your child will not want to cooperate. This section will discuss some common situations where children do not want to follow the rules of Time-Out and what you can do.

If your child misbehaves while he or she is in Time-Out, say nothing and ignore everything that is not dangerous to the child, yourself or others, and furniture.

> A child is about 18 months old when she figures out that the ball she rolled under the sofa will come out the other side.

Most negative behavior that occurs while a child is in Time-Out is an attempt to get you to react and say something, anything. Your child may whine, cry, complain, throw things, or make a big mess. He or she may make unkind comments about your parenting skills or say he or she doesn't love you anymore. This last one is perhaps the unkindest cut of all and, therefore, the hardest to ignore. Don't worry. Your child will love you again when the Time-Out is over.

When your child tries to leave Time-Out before time is up, it may be an attention-getting behavior, a sign that he or she is not developmentally ready for Time-Out, or because your child honestly needs time to calm down. In each instance, parents should use their judgment to decide how to help their children get through Time-Out.

For instance, if your child leaves Time-Out in order to get your attention, say absolutely nothing; just calmly and gently keep returning your child to Time-Out. If you need to interrupt Time-Out because of more pressing responsibilities, explain to your child what is happening and what will happen next. This might be a good time to use the mobile Time-Out, which is explained later in this section.

Young children often leave Time-Out because they are not developmentally ready for it; they think it is a game. If Time-Out isn't working, use smaller consequences like redo, undo, and redirect. (See Chapter 5.) These consequences take only a few seconds and can keep a young child's attention. In fact, these smaller consequences may actually prepare young children for bigger consequences like Time-Out, removing a privilege, or adding a chore.

Children might repeatedly leave Time-Out because they are too upset to control themselves. Parents should allow the child time to calm down before trying to start Time-Out again.

Initially, you may find that the more controlled and matter-of-fact you are about using Time-Out, the more agitated and out of control your children become. In other words, their behavior may get worse before it starts to get better. For some children, this spiraling experience is a part of how they must unlearn certain problem behaviors. It will take your patience, persistence, and ability to stay calm to help the household return to normal.

Perhaps the best things to do when children are crying or throwing a tantrum are to make sure they aren't in any danger and maintain a safe distance. Parents should briefly remind their kids to use some of the calming-down methods explained in Chapter 13 and occasionally check on their progress toward calming down.

When children lose self-control, parents need to switch gears, from trying to correct their children to helping them calm down. Try to remember that children will eventually learn through consistent teaching that no matter how long the tantrums last, their Time-Out does not go away.

Once your child is calm and quiet, you can tell him or her to go to Time-Out and that you have started the timer again. If you start the timer and the child continues to leave Time-Out or refuses to stop throwing a tantrum, you may decide that the behavior is too unruly for correction at that time and begin another parenting skill called *Teaching Self-Control.* (This skill will be explained later in this book.)

When your child is really able to control his or her emotions and behaviors, you can have him or her return to Time-Out and then start the timer again. Don't let your child learn that throwing a tantrum can get him or her out of Time-Out. If children are mature enough and have demonstrated that they understand how Time-Out works, parents can return them to Time-Out when they are calm.

You will know your children are calm when they can tell you they are calm. They also can show you they are calm if they can return to Time-Out without an argument.

Patience is the key to using Time-Out effectively. Your child may balk the first few times you use Time-Out, but he or she will eventually learn and accept your rules.

Using Time-Out Away from Home

Many parents will admit that half of their children's most embarrassing problem behaviors occur outside the home. When children misbehave in public, you should remain calm and quickly get your child to a quiet, isolated spot where you can sit down without interference to do Time-Out. You may want to identify a place where you can have some privacy and where the child won't be embarrassed or have an "audience" (a bench in the mall or a restroom hallway).

Some parents use a mobile Time-Out pad. This disk (the size of a dinner plate), which you can make out of paper or vinyl, can be folded up and carried in a pocket or purse. The small circular disk has two sides. One side has a sad face with "Time-Out" written on it. The other side has a smiling face. A parent places the sad face up and has the child sit or stand on it when he or she is in Time-Out. When Time-Out is over, the child gives the pad to the parent with the smiling face side showing.

It's best to teach children about how the Time-Out pad works before you do an actual Time-Out. This mobile Time-Out helps children understand that Time-Out can and will occur wherever they are and doesn't happen just at home. Some children may be able to go to Time-Out outside the home without using the pad; for other kids, using the pad may work better. Either way, the message is the same: Teaching goes on all the time and Time-Out can happen anywhere.

Just as at home, you should decide when your child is calm and quiet enough and is using the right behaviors to successfully complete a Time-Out. If a child is completely out of control, you may have to leave the area and help your child calm down. Then you can decide whether to do Time-Out or use another consequence.

Summing Up

Time-Out can be an effective consequence to help your young child learn what behaviors are unacceptable. Remember to use *Preventive Teaching* to help your son or daughter know what you expect of him or her in Time-Out. Keep in mind that the first few times your child earns a Time-Out, the consequence may not work or you may have mixed results. But with practice and consistency, your child soon will learn how the process works.

Some keys to increasing success with Time-Out include going over the steps to Time-Out to clearly show and tell your child what you expect, and practicing those steps with your child several times using *Preventive Teaching*. In addition, remember that the correcting and disciplining you do are teaching opportunities that will help your young child learn to do what's right.

[1] Eisenberg, A., Murkoff, H.E., & Hathaway, S.E. (1994). *What to expect: The toddler years*. New York: Workman Publishing.

Frequently Asked Questions
about
Time-Out

 "When should I use Time-Out?"

 Use Time-Out as a consequence with *Corrective Teaching,* which we will explain in Chapter 11. Immediately following a problem behavior, tell your child what he or she did wrong. Then take him or her to Time-Out.

For example, you might say, *"You must go to Time-Out because you just hit your sister."* Say this calmly and only once. Do not reason with or give long explanations to your child.

If your child does not go willingly, take him or her to Time-Out using as little force as needed. For example, hold the child gently by the hand or wrist and walk to the Time-Out area. Or, carry him or her facing away from you so that there is no confusion between a hug and a trip to Time-Out. Avoid giving your child a lot of attention as he or she is being put in Time-Out, and do not argue with, threaten, or spank your child.

Q "Where should the Time-Out area be?"

A You don't have to use the same place each time. Just make sure the place you choose is convenient for you and safe for the child. For example, using a downstairs chair is inconvenient when a problem behavior occurs upstairs. An adult-sized chair works best, but a step, footstool, bench, or couch also will work. Make sure the area is well lit and free of all dangerous objects. Also make sure your child cannot watch TV or play with toys while he or she is in Time-Out.

Q "How long should Time-Out last?"

A The upper limit should be one quiet minute for each year of your child's age. So if you have a 2-year-old, aim for two quiet minutes. Keep in mind, however, that every child is different; one 2-year-old may be perfectly able to sit quietly for two minutes, while another may barely be able to sit still for one minute.

Sometimes, it's better to set the time according to a child's developmental ability, rather than his or her age. The time can be adjusted as the child gets the hang of the rules and is able to sit quietly longer. This process may take time, especially at the beginning when children don't really understand why they need these rules and still don't believe you are really serious about using them.

Do not begin the time until your child is calm and quiet. If your child is crying or throwing a tantrum, it doesn't count toward his or her required time. If you start the Time-Out because your child is quiet but he or she starts to cry or throw a tantrum, wait until he or she is quiet before starting over again. Do not let your child leave Time-Out until he or she has calmed down. Your child must remain seated and be quiet to get out of Time-Out.

Some programs suggest using timers. Timers can be helpful but are not necessary. If you use one, remember that the timer is to remind parents, not children, that Time-Out is over. You're the one who told your child to go to Time-Out; you tell the child when it's over.

 "What counts as quiet time?"

You should decide what qualifies as calm and quiet behavior and explain it to your child. All kids are different. Some children get perfectly still and quiet while in Time-Out. Other children find it difficult to sit still and not talk. Fidgeting and "happy talk" should usually count as quiet time. For example, if your son sings or talks softly to himself, that counts as quiet time.

"What do I do when time is up?"

 When the Time-Out period is over, ask your child, *"Are you ready to get up?"* Your child must answer *"Yes"* in a way that is acceptable to you before you allow the child to get up. A simple *"Yes"* or a nod of the head should be sufficient.

 "If I try to put my son in Time-Out, he just blows up and has a tantrum. What should I do?"

 Keep in mind that Time-Out is a consequence and he is not going to like it, especially the first few times you use it. Do not give up. Your correction will work. Let him have his tantrum. Once it's over, put him back in Time-Out and remind him why he is there. It will probably be helpful to you and your son to practice how Time-Out works at a neutral time and let him practice it several times. Also, let your son know what behaviors will earn a Time-Out; then he'll know what to expect when he misbehaves. Children often find out on their own that tantrums won't be tolerated and that Time-Out keeps them away from doing fun things. If your child has frequent tantrums, read Chapter 13 on *Teaching Self-Control.*

11

Learning Right from Wrong

Dealing with Your Child's Misbehavior

* *

"Hey that's my toy!"

"I had it first – let go!"

"I'm going to tell Mom."

"You're a big fat baby!" (Child throws toy across the room and it breaks.)

"Mommy! Mommy! Mom!" (Child is crying and yelling.)

Sound familiar? For the parents of toddlers and pre-schoolers, squabbles like this can be part of daily life.

So far in this book, you have learned some wonderful tools that can help you prevent or reduce inappropriate behaviors. However, there are no parenting skills that can completely keep young children from misbehaving.

That's why the skill of *Corrective Teaching* is specifically designed to deal with misbehavior.

Corrective Teaching **is responding to your child's problem behavior by stopping the problem, and teaching and practicing positive alternatives.** *Corrective Teaching* combines steps you have already learned to help you respond consistently, effectively, and calmly to your child's problem behaviors.

There are five steps to *Corrective Teaching.* They are:

1. Show and Tell the problem behavior.
2. Give a negative consequence.
3. Show and Tell the desired behavior.
4. Give a reason.
5. Practice.

(These steps will be explained in detail later in this chapter.)

When to Use Corrective Teaching

It is best to start using *Corrective Teaching* with children (approximately 2 and older) when they are able to understand what consequences are. Match your teaching to your child's age and developmental level. For younger children, you may have to use one-word instructions or prompts and keep your teaching very short; older children can understand longer sentences and they have a longer attention span. Also remember that any teaching you do might not work right away or might not work all the time with your kids. It takes a lot of trial and error. But stay with it and keep working to improve your teaching skills.

> "A child is a curly, dimpled lunatic."
> — *Ralph Waldo Emerson*

We still encourage you to try to use small negative consequences like redo, undo, and redirect, along with *Show and Tell*, for most of your children's minor negative behaviors. When using *Corrective Teaching*, it is probably a good idea to use bigger consequences like Time-Out, removing a privilege, or adding a chore with children who are able to understand how the consequence works.

Usually, *Corrective Teaching* is effective with serious and/or frequent problem behaviors that fall into one of the following three categories:

Children DO NOT DO what they SHOULD DO.

There are many things you want your children to learn how to do: picking up their toys, putting on their shoes and socks, coming when called, sitting quietly, sharing, making an apology, staying near you, going to bed on time without arguing, and so on. When they don't do what they should do, *Corrective Teaching* can be used to teach them the importance of following through on your expectations.

Children DO what they SHOULDN'T DO.

Young children are naturally curious, adventuresome, self-centered, and independent-minded. This can often lead them to do things that aren't helpful or acceptable. Examples may include talking back, sneaking snacks, lying, breaking things, taking others' belongings, interrupting, getting into things, calling others names, etc. In situations like these, *Corrective Teaching* can be used to stop the problem behavior and teach children how to behave more appropriately.

Children do things that are POTENTIALLY DANGEROUS OR HARMFUL.

Sometimes, children act without thinking things through. This can lead to situations where they put themselves or others in danger of getting hurt or worse. Examples could include doing things like pulling a dog's tail, reaching for a hot stove, playing near the street, handling sharp objects, hitting or biting, throwing things, etc. In these situations, your first priority is to make sure everyone is safe and to tend to any injuries that might have occurred. Caring for your children and making sure they and others are safe (picking up glass from a broken window, taking a sharp knife away from a child who has gotten it out of a drawer, getting a child out of the street) also may give you time to think and get yourself calm before you start trying to correct their behavior. Once you're calm and the situation is safe, you can begin using *Corrective Teaching* to teach your child a better and safer way to behave.

Benefits of Corrective Teaching

It is important for parents to choose just one or two problem behaviors to work on at a time rather than trying to correct every behavior at once. *Corrective Teaching* helps parents do this. Parents and children can stay focused on working hard to change a behavior that is really disruptive before moving on to others. This is not to say you cannot correct other misbehaviors that pop up along the way. But when major problem behaviors appear, you can consistently correct them by using *Corrective Teaching*. This way, your child will get the message loud and clear that you

> "There is nothing as comforting as the patter of little children's feet about a home, because the moment the sound stops, you know they're doing something they shouldn't be."

will not tolerate certain behaviors. Agreeing on what to correct also helps parents develop similar tolerances (what will be accepted and what will not be accepted), and agree on a similar style of correction for misbehavior. To accomplish this goal, parents need to tell children what they did wrong and how to change their behavior.

Next, we'll discuss how to do *Corrective Teaching* with your children.

Steps of Corrective Teaching

Corrective Teaching uses steps that you learned earlier in this book to provide a simple, effective way to consistently respond to a child's problem behaviors. Here is an explanation of the steps of *Corrective Teaching*.

1. Show and Tell the problem behavior.

Young children often know when they have done something wrong. When their own feelings of guilt don't point it out, the look on a parent's face or the sound of a parent's voice can make it clear that they have made a mistake. However, we should never assume that our young children automatically know exactly what they have done wrong. We have to make sure they know what behavior we want them to change.

Showing and telling your child what he or she did wrong clearly defines the behavior you want the child to change. Showing and telling the problem behavior often begins with a description like *"You just..."* or *"I just heard you...."* Then, use simple words to describe the inappropriate behavior, such as, *"I just saw you hit your brother."*

Even if you do not see or hear what behaviors occurred, you can still use your ears and eyes to figure out what probably happened. For example, if two children come to you crying about a toy one of them had and the other took, you can determine what the problem behavior is and what type of correction it requires. At this point, you must decide whether to use a simple redo, undo, or redirect, or to start *Corrective Teaching*. If this is a major problem behavior that occurs frequently and seems to get worse each time, use *Corrective Teaching*.

2. Give a negative consequence.

As we mentioned earlier, negative consequences like Time-Out, removing a privilege, or adding a chore will work well in most *Corrective Teaching* situations. Remember to always use this step. Giving a consequence often begins with words like *"Because you did...."* This helps children see that they are receiving a consequence because they used a certain behavior.

3. Show and Tell the desired behavior.

Anytime you correct your children's behavior, your goal should be for things to get better in the future.

You must teach your children specifically and clearly how to behave. Showing and telling children the appropriate behavior they can do the next time teaches them how to prevent or avoid making similar mistakes in the future.

Even young children often know what they aren't supposed to do. To truly correct a problem, children need to know what they are supposed to do. Using words like *"Next time, you should..."* can help you get started on teaching positive alternatives. Oftentimes, you may teach a social skill that will help your child be more successful the next time a similar situation occurs.

4. Give a reason.

As mentioned earlier, reasons teach children what is likely to happen when they use certain behaviors. The reason should be age-appropriate, relate to the child, and be realistic, brief, and positive. Kid reasons may encourage your child to do the positive behavior you want more often in the future.

5. Practice.

You already know that young children learn and remember best by doing. Anytime we teach our children something, we want to have them practice. Having young children practice helps them establish positive behavior habits and allows every incident or correction to end with something positive and helpful. Try using the words *"Let's try..."* to help you get started on the practice step of *Corrective Teaching*. (Don't forget to praise your children for their attempts at practicing!) When children experience encouragement for doing the right thing, it increases the likelihood that they will do those things again in the future.

Correcting children does not have to be a situation that both parents and children dread. The steps of *Corrective Teaching* give parents a way to quickly and effectively teach children how to behave better in the future without forcing a test of wills. Read the following examples to see how quickly *Corrective Teaching* can occur and what it sounds like.

Example 1: Using Time-Out as a Consequence

1. **Show and Tell the problem behavior.**
   - Start with praise or empathy.
   - Specifically describe the behavior.
   - Be brief.

"I know you would like that toy, but you just grabbed it from your sister without asking and pushed her."

2. **Give a negative consequence.**
   - Contingent on the behavior.
   - Appropriate for the situation.

"For grabbing and pushing, you need to give me the toy and sit on the steps for four minutes in Time-Out." (Parent sets timer.) (After Time-Out is over.) *"Thanks for staying in Time-Out like I asked. Your time is up. You may get up."*

3. **Show and Tell the desired behavior.**
   - Label the skill.
   - Specifically describe the skill or behavior.

"Next time you want a toy your sister has, ask nicely by saying, 'May I please have a turn?'"

4. **Give a reason.**
   - Make it developmentally appropriate.
   - Be brief.

"If you ask nicely, your sister is more likely to share."

5. **Practice.**
   - Use pretend, play, or an actual situation.
   - Have the child actually do what was taught.
   - Be brief.

"Now, I'll hold the toy and you pretend that I am your sister. I want you to show me how you could ask for the toy. (Child practices by saying, "May I please have a turn?") Great job! You said 'Please' and asked to have a turn."

Example 2: Using Removing a Privilege as a Consequence . . . .

1. **Show and Tell the problem behavior.**

   "You were playing nicely a minute ago. Now you are being loud and arguing over this toy while I am talking on the phone."

2. **Give a negative consequence.**

   "I'm putting the toy up on the shelf until I am done talking."

3. **Show and Tell the desired behavior.**

   (Mom hangs up the phone.) *"When I am on the phone, you should sit here and use your quiet voices."*

4. **Give a reason.**

   "You can have play time while I'm on the phone if you use quiet voices."

5. **Practice.**

   "Now I am going to call my friend back. While I am talking to her, both of you can practice using your quiet voices."

179

Example 3: Using Undo as a Consequence ....

1. **Show and Tell the problem behavior.**

   "You make great pictures, but you are coloring on the wall when I've told you before not to do that."

2. **Give a negative consequence.**

   "You will help me clean the wall and straighten up in here." (Mom and child clean the wall.)

3. **Show and Tell the desired behavior.**

   "You should color only on the paper I give you."

4. **Give a reason.**

   "You get to keep your crayons if you color on paper."

5. **Practice.**

   "Show me how you can draw a pretty picture on this paper. (Child starts drawing on the paper.) *That's much better!"*

As you can see, correcting a child's behavior problems does not have to take very long. It simply means letting children know they are doing something you do not like and teaching them how to do what you do like. *Corrective Teaching* gives you a way to consistently do this.

Helpful Hints

Although correcting problem behaviors can often be simple and easy, we know this is not always the case. In fact, children sometimes make it quite challenging. To help you stay focused, keep in mind each of the following helpful hints.

Stay calm.

When your child is upset, that's a good cue for you to control your emotions. It may be helpful to have a *Staying Calm Plan,* which is described in Chapter 12. Although young children can be very stubborn and emotional, they truly take their cues from us. The better we are able to stay calm, the more likely it is that our children will stay calm.

Be brief.

Sometimes we think that the more we talk to our children, the more they learn. In fact, the opposite often is true; the more we talk, the less they hear. It should not take many words to let your children know what they did wrong and how to do better in the future. Keep it brief. Kids learn more from demonstration and practice than they do from words.

Be consistent.

Does it sometimes seem that you are correcting your child for the same thing over and over? Young children have short attention spans and memories. They truly forget things as fast as we can teach them. That's why it is important for parents to be consistent with rules, routines, and correcting behavior. Consistency reminds young children what the limits are, what is acceptable, and what is not.

> "Before I got married, I had six theories about bringing up children. Now I have six children and no theories."
>
> – *John Wilmot*

Look for cooperation.

Young children can be very busy. They seem to move from one problem behavior to another and they take us right along with them. However, parents do not want it to always be this way. When our children make mistakes, we want to encourage them to turn their behavior around and make a positive start. We can help this to occur by praising good behaviors even when our children make mistakes. For example, if a child teases a playmate, a parent can praise the child for stopping the teasing when told, coming to the parent when asked, listening while being corrected, going to Time-Out and staying there, practicing how to get along better, or making an apology. Looking for and praising cooperation can help take some of the struggle out of correcting a problem.

Use kid reasons.

Just like with other parenting skills, using kid reasons may help your children better understand what you expect and encourage them to try what you have taught them.

Stick to one issue.

Children are masterful at getting us off track. No matter what the original issue may be, children can quickly get us turned around with statements like *"You don't love me," "But, he did it first,"* or *"Daddy said I could."* Young children also can muddy the water with tears, yelling, naughty words, or sneaky tricks like giving us a hug or kiss in the middle of being corrected. Whatever they do, it is important that you still correct your children for the inappropriate behavior. You can always address other issues later. If kids continue to whine, pout, argue, or cry, you may need to give them time to calm down.

Summing Up

Correcting child behavior problems is rarely something parents look forward to doing. However, as long as children make mistakes, it will always remain part of rearing children.

It's important, though, to not look at responding to our children's problems behaviors merely as an unpleasant chore. It is much more than that. It is a wonderful opportunity – an opportunity to teach our children how to be more successful, an opportunity to make our lives easier by correcting a problem now before it becomes a bigger problem, an opportunity to show our children that we care too much to allow them to continue to make poor choices, an opportunity to show our children that even when they make a mistake, we will still treat them with respect and love.

Corrective Teaching is a tool that can help us "get through" a problem situation, teach our children how to do what's right, and strengthen our families.

Frequently Asked Questions about
Corrective Teaching

"How do I correct a 4-year-old for biting?"

When children are frustrated, they will sometimes use aggressive behaviors such as biting. You should stop the child's behavior immediately, then briefly describe the misbehavior. *("No biting. It hurts people.")* It is important to use a firm voice tone and follow up with a consequence that you can consistently use, like Time-Out, removing a privilege, or undoing a behavior. Be sure to teach what you want your child to do instead of biting.

"Sometimes I correct my children for things they do wrong but they do it again. How can I keep from having to correct them all the time?"

Misbehavior in young children is a natural learning experience. The key to changing or stopping it is consistency. Make sure you use effective and logical consequences and check to see that your expectations are reasonable. Be patient and look for any improvements in your children's behavior. When you see even a slight improvement, make sure you use *Effective Praise* (Chapter 7).

"My daughter just ignores everything I say when I correct her because she knows her dad will let her have whatever she wants. How can I deal with this?"

 Sit down and talk with your spouse about the differences in your parenting styles. Reach an agreement on how you both will correct your child in one particular area. Once you both have been able to work together on smaller issues, work on reaching an agreement for handling bigger issues. Being consistent is a key to successful parenting.

 "I do want to be more consistent about correcting my children. But do I have to correct every little thing they do?"

 Don't sweat the small stuff. Correcting every little thing can cause the quality and consistency of your teaching to decline. Small problems can be redirected, done over, or undone, while frequent and severe problem behaviors need more correction. Choose a few problem behaviors that really upset you and work on correcting them. In other words, pick your battles. Constant correction will be seen as nagging and can actually result in more negative behavior.

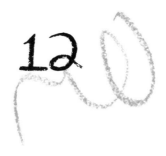

Take a Deep Breath...

Making a Plan to Stay Calm

* *

M any parents tell us that the biggest challenge they
face in dealing with their child's problem behaviors is staying calm. Young children can be constantly
active, asking questions, making messes, throwing temper tantrums, or just basically doing a lot of things that
cause trouble. In order to prepare for this barrage of
behavior, parents need to keep their cool.

Please understand that we are not saying you won't get
angry. That's impossible, maybe even unhealthy, since
anger is a basic human emotion. We are simply saying
that blowing your top over your child's behavior can
make situations worse.

When we ask parents what they do when they are
angry, some say they yell at or grab their kids. Some say

they hit something or throw or kick things. Many parents are totally convinced that these angry responses work to show their kids they "mean business." And they are right. These responses do temporarily stop the problem behavior. But what did their children learn? To yell, hit, throw or kick things when they are upset.

In this chapter, we lay out a parent's plan for staying calm. There are three steps to developing your *Staying Calm Plan:*

1. Identify what your kids do that gets you upset.

2. Identify what you are doing or feeling that signals you are getting upset.

3. Decide what you are going to do instead of getting upset in the future.

Step 1: What Upsets You

Knowing what makes us angry is the first step in being able to respond calmly to our kids' problem behaviors. Typically, kids are able to push our buttons and say the words or do the actions that get under our skin.

On a piece of paper, list the specific behaviors your kids have done in the past that resulted in you losing your temper. Pay attention to what your kids said, what they did, what voice tone they used, and so on. Also, it will help to identify the situations in which these behaviors occur. For example, did this annoying behavior occur after you gave your children an instruction, corrected them, or asked them to help around the house? Or did it happen at a certain time of day, such as before meals or at bedtime? The more specific you are when making this list, the more successful you're likely to be in calmly facing these situations in the future.

Step 2: Your Warning Signs

There are a whole series of feelings that flood our bodies when we start to get upset. Our behavior also changes. At these times, how you deal with these feelings makes all the difference in what you do or say. If you lose control and say or do everything that's racing through your mind, you'll only make the situation worse, hurt your kids' feelings, and regret it later. In other words, good things rarely happen when you get upset with your kids and lose self-control.

> "You can't be too careful what you tell a child because you never know what he'll take hold of and spend the rest of his life remembering you by."
>
> – *Frederick Buechner*

We all have little signals that show we're getting angry. Recognizing these "red flags" allows us to think before we act. It's much easier to work our way through a problem when we can remain calm.

What are your "red flags"? Does your heart race or your face get flushed? Do you clench your teeth, make a fist, or feel your muscles tighten? Do you talk faster or louder or start pointing and making abrupt movements?

> "There is nothing more influential in a child's life than the moral power of a quiet example."
>
> – William Bennett

Take some time to think about the early warning signs that indicate you're beginning to get upset. Before you can change how you respond to your kids, you have to know exactly what your anger signs are. On the sheet of paper where you listed your kids' behavior, write down the things you do or feel when you're beginning to get angry.

Step 3: Make a Plan

Now, let's take a look at how you can use these signals to help you stay calm in tense situations with your children. What we're going to do is combine:

* Your child's problem behaviors, and

* Your early warning signals, with

* A way of staying calm that works for you.

Here is an example of how one parent used these three pieces to make her *Staying Calm Plan*.

Example

When **Johnny talks back to me and refuses to go to bed** *(child's problem behaviors)*, and I start feeling **my heart pound** *(my warning sign)*, I will **take a deep breath and let it out slowly** *(what I will do)* to calm down.

Staying calm wasn't easy for this parent, at first. She had to work at it. But the more she concentrated on her plan, the more successful she was at staying calm. She said she felt better about the way she interacted with her son and almost felt a sense of pride in being able to maintain her self-control.

Here are some ways that other parents have told us they calm down in tense situations:

* *"I count to ten – very slowly. I concentrate on doing that regardless of what my son is yelling."*

* *"I put my hands in my pockets. I tend to be really demonstrative with my hands, especially when I'm angry. Before I learned to do this, I think my daughter thought I was going to hit her. I wasn't, but she viewed my behavior as a threat."*

* *"I sit down. If I'm standing, I begin to tremble. Sitting calms me for some reason. I can still tell my child what he's doing wrong, but I say it a lot more calmly."*

* *"I take a deep breath and let it out slowly. This serves as a safety valve for me. It's like I'm letting steam out of my body."*

* *"I just leave the situation for a while. I go in another room until I can calm myself. I figure if my kid's that mad, taking a little time to regain my self-control won't hurt anything. I can deal with it a lot better that way. Sometimes, he even calms down by the time I get back."*

* *"This may sound crazy, but I wear a rubber band on my wrist and snap the band whenever I feel like I'm getting upset. That's a signal to myself that I'd better calm down."*

* *"I used to get so upset with my 5-year-old that the only thing I found that helped me calm down was to wash my face with cool water."*

* *"I call someone like my best friend or my sister. By talking about the situation, I can go back in and deal with it more calmly."*

* *"I sit down and on paper write about how upset I am. Sometimes, I can't even read what I've written. That's not as important as the fact that I'm not taking it out on my son. When I calm down, I'm always surprised at how upset I got over such a little thing."*

On the same piece of paper you listed your child's behaviors and your anger warning signs, add the finishing touches by writing a plan for yourself. Parents tell us that when they write out their plan, they are more likely to remember it and use it during a real situation. Make it look something like this:

When _____ ,

(child's problem behavior)

and I start feeling _____ ,

(my warning signals)

I will _____**to calm down.**

(what I will do to stay calm)

Helpful Hints

Learning to control your negative reactions will take some time. Don't get discouraged if you lose your temper every now and then. Here are some tips that have helped other parents:

Practice positive self-talk.

If you find yourself thinking negative thoughts, interrupt those thoughts. Say "Stop it!" to yourself. Then refocus on positive thoughts. It helps you keep your self-control and work through whatever problem you're dealing with.

Here are some examples of positive self-talk other parents have used:

"Relax. Take it easy."

"I am going to help my child."

"Take it slowly."

"I'm a good parent, and I can do this."

"It's going to get better. It just takes time."

You will find that the more often you use positive self-talk, the better you will feel about yourself and your role as a parent. Even if you don't see any immediate change in your child's behavior, you can certainly prevent the problem from getting worse.

Negative, self-defeating thoughts always lead to more problems. By using positive self-talk, you not only learn to control your emotions, but also are able to better concentrate on the task at hand – teaching your children positive ways to behave.

Don't take what your child says personally.

This may be very difficult when your child is calling you names or saying hurtful things. You must convince yourself that your child does this because he or she hasn't yet acquired the skills necessary to deal with anger or frustration. Don't react when you get called a name or when you are accused of being a rotten parent. Learn how to let negative, angry comments bounce off you and the effectiveness of your teaching will increase.

Use the 'take five' rule.

Instead of blurting out an angry response, tell yourself to take five minutes to think about what is happening. It is remarkable how that "cooling off" period can help a person regain self-control and put things in perspective. Simply leaving the situation sometimes can help to "defuse" a volatile situation.

> "There is just one way to bring up a child in the way he should go and that is to travel that way yourself."
>
> – Abraham Lincoln

Focus on behavior, not motives.

Instead of looking for the reasons for your child's negative behavior, deal with the way he or she is acting. You can drive yourself batty trying to figure out why your child is misbehaving. After the problem is solved, take the time to talk to your child about what happened and why.

If you lose control, say you're sorry.

If you get angry and say or do something you regret, go back to your child and say you're sorry. This models for your children what they should do when they make a mistake. Apologize, say what you did wrong, and say what you're going to do differently next time. Apologizing makes parents more "human," too. Kids sometimes feel that parents are always right, no matter what happens. Admitting a mistake often is the best thing you can do. Then do your best not to let it happen again.

Use a firm voice.

Staying calm does not mean you are totally passive. There are times when you will raise your voice, but use a firm, no-nonsense voice tone. Make sure the words you use are specific descriptions, not judgments, put-downs, or expressions of your negative feelings. Staying calm means you don't react to misbehavior in an angry, aggressive manner.

Summing Up

Staying calm and maintaining self-control is the key to effective teaching and parenting. Making a *Staying Calm Plan* for yourself gives you a consistent way to calm yourself when your child's behaviors make you angry or upset. Remember these steps and follow through with them.

1. Look at your own behavior.

2. Identify what makes you angry.

3. Know what you are going to say and do to calm down.

4. Control negative responses and deal with them quickly.

13

...And Count to Ten!

Teaching Your Child Self-Control

* *

You are in a grocery store. You hear a loud crash directly in front of you and you see a dozen cans of green beans scatter across the floor. In the middle of the mess is a small boy sprawled on the floor clutching a half-eaten candy bar. His mother is trying to wrestle the candy from him, but he is kicking and screaming and yelling, "My candy!" His mother tells him to be quiet, but it only makes him scream louder. "No I won't!" he yells. "And you can't make me."

How would you handle a situation like this with your child? All parents of young children have experienced frustration when their child throws a tantrum. Children may whine, cry, hit, bite, yell, stomp their feet, argue, or throw things. On the other side of the emotional scale, children may refuse to talk or follow instructions, close their eyes tightly, hide from or ignore their parents, or hold their breath to the point of fainting. Regardless of the behavior, these children are out of their parents' control. That can cause parents to feel angry, embarrassed, or helpless. Emotional outbursts or stubborn defiance by children are difficult to handle, and parents need a positive way to respond so their children learn self-control.

In this chapter, you will learn how to help your kids when negative emotions get the best of them. We call this parenting skill *Teaching Self-Control.*

A Learned Behavior

Many parents don't understand why their children sometimes get so out of control. Some parents even think that they are doing a terrible job of rearing their kids and take the "acting out" behaviors personally, as if such a display was a sign of their children's dislike for them. At those times, parents need to remind themselves that acting out is a negative behavior, and like all behaviors, it is learned.

Almost anything can trigger a child's loss of self-control. Very young children usually act out because they are hungry, tired, or frustrated. Often, they can't tell their parents what is wrong and this frustration boils over into negative behavior. Just think if you were unable to let others know what you were feeling. It would make you mad, too. As kids get older, however, they've probably learned that these tantrums or defiant acts can get them something they want or allow them to avoid something they don't like.

Most parents and their kids go through some very similar scenes: Kids throw a tantrum and parents get worn down. Sometimes, parents just get tired of the aggravation and disruption that comes from hearing the crying, whining, and screaming.

> "Give to a pig when it grunts and a child when it cries, and you will have a fine pig and a bad child."
>
> – Danish proverb

Other times, parents are so embarrassed that they just want to give the child something so he or she will be quiet, especially if a child is having a tantrum in public. Often, kids act out simply to get attention – yours or anyone else's. They figure that negative attention is better than none at all. Regardless of the reasons, it is very important to handle these disruptive behaviors consistently, correctly, and calmly.

As you've learned in this book, your usual response to negative behavior is to use *Corrective Teaching*. And you need to be persistent and in control of your emotions when you use it. (Remember to use the *Staying Calm Plan* we talked about earlier.) This teaching method works well for most minor misbehaviors. However, when a child escalates defiance or acting out to the point where he or she won't follow any instructions and is not responding to your teaching, it's time to change your approach. It's time to use *Teaching Self-Control*.

Teaching Self-Control **is a parent's calm response to a child's emotional outburst or continued refusal to behave so that important teaching can take place.** There are two parts to *Teaching Self-Control*. The first part is called *Calming Down* and consists of these steps:

Part 1

1. Show and Tell the problem behavior.
2. Describe the desired behavior.
3. Allow time to calm down.
4. Check for cooperative behavior.

The second part of *Teaching Self-Control* is called *Follow-Up Teaching*. It includes the following steps:

Part 2

5. Show and Tell the desired behavior (Stay Calm).
6. Give a reason.
7. Practice (Stay Calm).
8. Show approval.

We can't totally prevent acting out and defiance by our children. However, we can try to help our kids get through these outbursts without having a major battle erupt. *Teaching Self-Control* uses steps you have already learned in previous skills to guide you through these out-of-control situations. Let's take a look at when you should use this powerful teaching tool.

When to Use Teaching Self-Control

First, you should take every precaution to avoid using *Teaching Self-Control* too frequently. Pay attention to events that lead up to tantrums and defiance. You know when your children are most likely to act out. It's a good habit to assess the circumstances – time of day, people who are present, activity being done, result of the behavior, etc. – that surround a tantrum or a stubborn stretch of defiance. You may find that some of these episodes can be prevented. For example, if it's about time for a child's nap or if the child is hungry, it may not be a good time to go to the grocery store. Postpone the trip if you can and wait until a better time or heck to see if a game or puzzle is too difficult for your child's ability; the frustration of not being able to do something correctly may build until he or she explodes. Check whether negative behavior is being strengthened by the way people respond to it. If kids are getting what they want by acting out, then they probably will continue to act out.

Use *Preventive Teaching* frequently to set some guidelines and expectations for positive behavior, no matter where you're going or what activity you are doing. Before problem situations occur, think of consequences you can use, let your child know what they are and when they will be used, and stick with them. Don't treat out-of-control behavior as an isolated event coming out of nowhere. There are reasons for the behavior, and it may benefit you and your child to always note what happens before and after your child loses control.

But try as you might, there will be times when nothing seems to work. Generally, parents tell us that they most often use *Teaching Self-Control* in two primary situations:

* When children respond to *Corrective Teaching* with defiance or refusal

* When children use sudden, emotional, intense behaviors

When children respond to *Corrective Teaching* with defiance or refusal.

Many times, young children respond very well to redirection, teaching, and correction. However, there are times when it is difficult for them to accept or respond to their parents' instructions. Your children could react with stubbornness, impatience, embarrassment, anger, defiance, or some other emotion that interferes with your teaching. They may whine, cry, stomp their feet, argue, or simply ignore you. Whatever they do, your children are showing you they will not listen to reason and are not ready for your teaching. This is not the time to continue using *Corrective Teaching*; instead, begin using *Teaching Self-Control*.

What are some behaviors your child does when he or she gets upset and refuses to do what you ask? Make a list.

> "Children have never been very good at listening to their elders, but they have never failed to imitate them."
>
> – *James Baldwin*

When children use sudden, emotional, intense behaviors.

Sometimes, children have an uncontrollable outburst of emotion or defiance. This behavior is so intense that it calls for your immediate response. Children might hurt other people or damage things, scream at the top of their lungs, call people names, throw toys or clothes, kick the dog, or display other dramatic, intense, negative behaviors. You may have no clue why your child is acting out, but the first goal should be to get your child calmed down so you can find out what happened and then respond correctly.

When your child suddenly becomes out of control, there are several things to think about before you decide to use *Teaching Self-Control*. It could be that your child is afraid or frightened, hurt, or sad. Although these emotions may trigger some kind of acting-out behavior, they first require a nurturing response instead of a teaching response.

For example, what should you do if you pick your son up from day care and he begins to cry and will not be comforted no matter what you do? It would be wise to first ask the day care staff what happened (if your child won't tell you) and make sure your child is okay. Maybe one of the other kids bit or hit him, or he feels rejected and left out. This would require a comforting and soothing response. On the other hand, if your child started screaming and crying when he saw you walk in the door simply because he didn't want to stop playing with the other kids, that would require a *Corrective Teaching* response. And if *Corrective Teaching* didn't stop the problem behavior, then it's time to move to *Teaching Self-Control*.

There also are safety issues to consider. A young child's emotions can be very intense. Children can become extremely angry or feel a tremendous need to let out whatever they are feeling. Unfortunately, most young children don't know appropriate ways to express these emotions; they don't know when to stop or don't always understand the consequences of their actions. This can lead to dangerous behaviors like head banging, biting, hitting, throwing things, pushing, breaking things, or running away from you. Children can direct these outbursts at other children, parents, or even themselves.

At these times, do what you can to make the situation safe (remove any harmful objects from your child's reach, get other children out of the area, remove your child from the area) before you try to calm your child down or do any teaching. Once you know your child and others are safe and have determined that you need to use *Teaching Self-Control*, the first step is to make sure you are calm and able to handle the situation.

The Importance of Staying Calm

It's not unusual for parents to lose their cool over their children's behavior. Parents can feel frustration and anger, or they can simply get tired of having to deal with their child's emotional outbursts or other serious misbehaviors. Or maybe parents are overstressed at work or home and their patience has worn thin. Whatever the case, parents also may feel like yelling, screaming, and throwing things sometimes. It's very normal to feel this way. But acting on these feelings is not a good idea, especially around your young children. At those volatile times, you absolutely must recognize what you're feeling and do something constructive to get yourself calmed down so you can teach your kids.

We've discussed this in earlier chapters, but it is worth repeating again: **Staying calm is the key to effective teaching and effective parenting.** If you have a difficult time controlling your own emotions, practice what you listed in your *Staying Calm Plan* (Chapter 12). Some parents really have to work hard at finding and using constructive ways to settle down when their kids are acting out. But after they find a healthy way to remain calm, the benefits to their kids and themselves are dramatic.

In the next section, we'll talk about the specific steps of *Teaching Self-Control.*

Part 1: Calming Down

Kids aren't receptive to teaching when they are out of control and their negative emotions and behaviors are running wild. Therefore, before any teaching can be done, your child has to be calm enough to listen to you and follow instructions.

These steps make up the *Calming Down* phase of *Teaching Self-Control*:

1. Show and Tell the problem behavior.

2. Describe the desired behavior.

3. Allow time to calm down.

4. Check for cooperative behavior.

1. Show and Tell the problem behavior.

Many times, youngsters are so focused on their emotions or the situation at hand that they aren't aware of (or don't care about) their behavior. That's when it's important to accurately let them know what they are doing wrong. What you say or do should be brief, specific, and to the point without sounding sarcastic or belittling. It's also helpful to start with praise or empathy.

A good example might be simply saying, *"I know you are upset, but you are yelling and screaming."* Then your child knows specifically what the problem is. But saying (as many of us have done occasionally), *"I want you to quit that right now! You're acting like a big baby!"* is vague and ineffective. It works much better to simply give brief, accurate statements that describe the behavior.

Other suggestions to help you describe the problem behavior include using a calm voice and saying things in a direct, no-nonsense manner. You also could show that you understand how your child feels (empathy) by using phrases like *"I know that made you mad,"* or *"I know how upset you are right now."* Describing behavior in these ways makes it easier for your child to grasp what you're saying and lets him or her know you care. You help your kids see their own behavior (and your disapproval) without having to raise your voice or lose your temper.

2. Describe the desired behavior.

When your child isn't able to get a handle on his or her emotions, you will need to briefly and specifically describe or demonstrate how to calm down and stay calm. For example, you can say, *"On the count of three, let's take a deep breath to calm down. Ready? One, two, three...."* In some cases, you may have already taught and practiced with your child (through *Preventive Teaching*) how to use a calm-down method. These methods could include having the child take a deep breath or focus on some object in the room until he or she feels calm. Other prompts might include counting to 5 or 10, or hugging a stuffed animal or pillow. This is a very good time to use the methods and ideas we discussed in *Preventive Teaching* (Chapter 9). If you teach your children these methods in advance, they will have a better idea of what they should do when they find themselves getting angry or upset.

At other times, your descriptions should be geared toward redirecting your child and stopping the negative behavior. For example, you can say, *"Please stop screaming,"* or *"Please hold your legs still instead of kicking the wall."*

There will be times when your child won't immediately calm down. His or her emotions may still be in control and the misbehavior could get worse before it gets better. That's a very common response for young children. In fact, they often will raise the intensity of their behavior until parents give up or give in. When parents respond this way, it actually makes the negative behavior stronger, and the child is more likely to use the behavior in other situations because he or she has learned that it works in making parents back off. Kids think, *"If I turn it up a notch here, Mom will go away and I won't have to deal with her."* So, remember to stick to the steps of *Teaching Self-Control* and give a clear description or demonstration of the desired behavior of calming down when you see your child beginning to lose it. This plants the seeds for more acceptable behavior.

> "A toddler believes that if you love a person, you will stay with that person 100 percent of the time."
>
> — *Lawrence Balter*

Please realize it may take numerous tantrums and frequent teaching before your message sinks in and your kids learn to follow your prompts for calming down and regaining self-control. The keys to helping your child calm down are staying calm yourself and being patient.

3. Allow time to calm down.

This step is a safeguard for both you and your child. If your child will not cooperate or follow instructions and the negative behavior is careening out of control, he or she needs a chance to calm down. You do too. Parents can make situations worse by responding to extremely negative behaviors with negative behaviors of their own. This only serves to fuel the fire. Resorting to screaming at your child, hitting or spanking, making threats, or giving unreasonable or ridiculous consequences (taking all the child's toys away or saying Time-Out will last for five hours) will not help.

Most times, it's best for you and your child to just go to "neutral corners." The purpose is to take a break from one another until you both settle down. This doesn't mean leaving the child completely alone or unmonitored. You have to be able to ensure that nothing worse can happen. Make sure you can still monitor your child and occasionally check to see if he or she is safe and starting to calm down. **NEVER LEAVE A VERY YOUNG, OUT-OF-CONTROL CHILD UNATTENDED.**

Even if your child is still screaming when he or she follows your instruction to go where you say, that's the beginning of the calming-down process. However, if your child refuses, you might need to take him or her there gently. If your child is already in a place that you consider calm and safe, you might leave the immediate area until your child is calmer.

It may take a few minutes or it may take a lot longer for your child to calm down. Take advantage of this break to calm yourself down. Don't dwell on what your child has said or take the behavior personally. Instead, concentrate on your own *Staying Calm Plan*. Once you're calm, think about how you want to continue.

4. Check for cooperative behavior.

Periodically go back to your child and check on how calm or cooperative he or she is. One of the easiest ways to check whether or not children are calm is to see if they are ready to follow one or two simple instructions, such as looking at you, coming to sit beside you, or listening without interrupting. You could say, *"Please look at me"* or *"Please sit down over here,"* or ask, *"Are you ready to talk to me now?"* When children are not able to do what you ask, they probably need more time to calm down before you can teach them. If your child can successfully follow instructions, you can go to *Follow-Up Teaching*, the next part of *Teaching Self-Control*.

The steps we have covered may seem like a lot to do during a very difficult time. However, these steps can be done relatively easily. (The time it takes to do this part could vary from a few minutes to much longer, depending on how quickly your child is able to calm down.) Read the following example to see how the *Calming Down* part of *Teaching Self-Control* might sound. (This parent has already attempted *Corrective Teaching*, but because the child's behavior got so intense so quickly, she decided to start *Teaching Self-Control*.)

Situation: Child stomps feet and yells when told he can't have some candy

1. **Show and Tell the problem behavior.**
   - Start with praise or empathy.
   - Describe the out-of-control behavior.

   "I know you're disappointed. But right now you are yelling and stomping your feet." (Parent demonstrates child's stomping.)

2. **Describe the desired behavior.**
   - Specifically describe or demonstrate how to calm down.
   - Be brief.

   "Please stop. Why don't you take a deep breath to calm down?" (Parent demonstrates taking a deep breath.)

3. **Allow time to calm down.**
   - Allow space.
   - Allow time.
   - Monitor.

   "I'm going to give you a few minutes to work on calming yourself down. Please go to your room and I'll check on you later."

4. Check for cooperative behavior.

- Give a simple instruction.

(A few minutes later.) *"Are you ready to listen now? (Child nods head.) Okay. Why don't you come over here and let's talk."*

Part 2: Follow-Up Teaching

During the *Follow-Up Teaching* phase of *Teaching Self-Control*, your primary goal is to use the following steps to teach your child how to stay calm in future situations:

5. Show and Tell the desired behavior (Stay Calm).

6. Give a reason.

7. Practice (Stay Calm).

8. Show approval.

5. Show and Tell the desired behavior (Stay Calm).

Just as you *Show and Tell* the problem behavior in Part 1, it's important to *Show and Tell* the desired behavior in Part 2. Again, start with praise or empathy and specifically describe or demonstrate how to stay calm. It may sound something like this: *"Good job coming to sit by me when I asked. When you are mad, instead of yelling and stomping, take some deep breaths like this* (demonstrate) *to stay calm."*

6. Give a reason.

Giving a reason for why it's important to stay calm can help a young child understand why this behavior is important. You may say something like, *"When you stay calm, you won't get into as much trouble."*

7. Practice (Stay Calm).

As with all the teaching tools you have learned, practicing will help your child be more successful at staying calm in the future. For example, you could say, *"Let's pretend you are upset about a toy being broken. Take three really deep breaths with me. Ready, here we go... One, two, three"* (breathing together).

8. Show approval.

Finally, you will end the interaction with approval so your child is more likely to use the Staying Calm skill in the future. While giving your child a hug, you could say, *"You did a really good job of practicing how to Stay Calm!"*

Read the following example to see how the *Follow-Up* part of *Teaching Self-Control* might sound in the situation with the child who stomped his feet and yelled when he was told he couldn't have some candy. (Again, the parent has already attempted *Corrective Teaching*, but because the child's behavior got so intense so quickly, she decided to start *Teaching Self-Control*.)

Example

5. Show and Tell the desired behavior (Stay Calm).	*"I know it's hard to stay calm when you can't have some candy. But instead of yelling and stomping, how about counting to 10?"*
• Start with praise or empathy.	
• Specifically describe or demonstrate how to stay calm.	
6. Give a reason.	*"If you can stay calm by counting to 10 instead of yelling and stomping, you might get some candy later."*
• Make it developmentally appropriate.	
• Be brief.	
7. Practice (Stay Calm).	*"Okay, let's practice counting to 10 together. Ready? 1, 2, 3, 4, 5...."*
• Use pretend, play, or an actual situation.	
• Have the child actually do what was taught.	
• Be brief.	
8. Show approval.	*"Wow, that was a great practice counting to stay calm. Big kiss for you!"*
• Give a praise statement.	
• Smile, hug, touch.	

Follow-Up Teaching allows parents to help their child make positive changes following an emotional outburst.

Each time parents follow up an emotional situation with teaching, they help their children move one step closer toward understanding that they must learn to control their emotions and that their behaviors will not deter parents from eventually teaching them what they need to learn.

Keys to Effectively Teaching Self-Control

Here are some keys to keep in mind when using *Teaching Self-Control.*

> "The quickest way for a parent to get a child's attention is to sit down and look comfortable."
>
> — *Lane Olinghouse*

* **Focus on Time-In.** Parents should spend time with their children doing fun things so they will see that good behavior gets most of their parents' time and attention. If children receive most of their parents' attention and time when they are upset or having a tantrum, they will be more likely to do those behaviors, no matter what the price.

* **Stay calm.** The calmer parents can be, the easier it is for young children to calm down. Use your *Staying Calm Plan* to remain calm.

* **Allow all the time that is needed.** *Calming Down* does not work well when it is rushed. Give your children and yourself as much time as you need to calm down.

* **Make sure to use Follow-Up Teaching.** This will help to encourage improvements, allow additional practice, discourage future tantrums, or accomplish another of your teaching goals.

* **Use kid reasons.** Kid reasons can be used to show children that tantrums aren't helpful and why calming down quickly is a better choice.

* **Plan ahead.** All children (and parents) will occasionally become emotional. Use *Preventive Teaching* often to set your child up for success in all situations. Also use *Preventive Teaching* to practice ways to calm down.

Helpful Hints

The most difficult part of *Teaching Self-Control* is having to use it when your child's emotions (and maybe your own) are running high. To help you handle these stressful situations effectively, keep in mind the following helpful hints:

Be aware of your physical actions.

What you do is often more powerful than what you say. As you try to help guide your children toward calming down, it is important that you do not distract or scare them with angry facial expressions, loud voice tones, or sharp gestures. Remember, everything you do when you are angry gives your children "permission" to do the same things when they are angry.

Look for cooperation.

Just as in *Corrective Teaching*, use praise and encouragement to help children turn things around after they have struggled. Parents can encourage children for trying their calming-down strategies, taking time to calm themselves, calming down more quickly than usual, practicing during the *Follow-Up Teaching*, making apologies, accepting consequences, and making other efforts to get back on track.

Keep your expectations reasonable.

It's normal for a young child to whine or be stubborn at times. Don't expect complete obedience. Children are constantly testing limits; it's part of their development. Set limits ahead of time and explain these rules in simple language. The number of rules you have for your child should increase according to your child's age and ability to understand and perform a behavior. Some minor misbehaviors can simply be ignored. Others can be gently and firmly dealt with and then they're over quickly. But don't make "a mountain out of a molehill" by expecting your child to do something he or she is not able to do.

Give your child a gentle reminder before changing routines or rules, such as when dinner will be ready or when he or she needs to get ready for bed. Kids like the comfort of a routine and abruptly interrupting that routine can cause some kids to throw a tantrum. Saying things like *"We're going to eat in 10 minutes. Why don't you start putting your toys away now?"* gives your child a chance to adjust to a new expectation.

When nothing seems to work.

If you have consistently and calmly used *Teaching Self-Control* techniques but your child continues having frequent and violent tantrums (especially after the age of 4) or has hurt himself or herself or others, talk to your pediatrician to make sure there are no serious physical or psychological problems triggering the behavior.

Additional Parenting Tools for Calming Kids

Teaching Self-Control is a tool parents should use to help children calm down and teach them how to stay calm in future situations. Since no two children are alike, and different approaches may work better with some children, you may want to try using some of these other parenting tools:

Redirect: Involve your child in another constructive activity. *"Why don't you help me put the groceries away?"*

Redo/Overlearn: Have your child appropriately repeat an action or statement he or she did incorrectly. *"Would you say 'Okay' after I tell you 'No'? Let's try it."*

Undo: Reverse or correct the effects of a negative behavior. *"Say, 'Daddy, I'm sorry for screaming.'"*

Time-Out: Remove your child from fun things for a short, quiet period. *"Because you screamed and stomped your feet for so long, you'll need to go to Time-Out for three minutes."*

Practice Calming Skills: Rehearse one of the skills you have taught your child during *Preventive Teaching.* *"Let's practice taking a deep breath for when you start getting upset."*

Practice Social Skills: Teach a behavior that could help your child avoid getting frustrated or angry and prevent the problem behavior from occurring. *"Let's practice how to accept 'No.'"*

Additional Consequences: Remove a privilege or possession for a short period of time. *"You can't have a snack until Mommy says it's time."*

Return to the Original Issue: Ask your child what happened to cause the outburst and together find ways to correct it in the future. *"Let's talk about why you got so mad."*

Don't be surprised if you use more than one skill or tool at a time to help your children improve their behavior. It's sometimes easy to "piggyback" these options because they can be completed in a short time.

It's also not unusual for parents of one child to choose options that are different from those used by parents of another child, even when the children did the same thing. It all depends on what the parents believe their child needs to learn most. Let's look at an example.

A boy bites his sister during an argument over a toy they both want. One parent might choose to immediately put the boy in Time-Out, firmly say, *"Don't bite. It hurts people,"* and then give his attention to his daughter. Another parent might want to teach the boy the skill of apologizing by having him tell his sister he is sorry (teach a social skill), and then having him offer to do something nice to make up for biting her. Another parent might remove a possession or activity from the boy, such as taking away the toy that originally caused the conflict and putting it in Time-Out (additional consequences). And another parent might concentrate on helping the boy practice calming-down strategies.

As you can see, a parent's tolerances and point of view play a big part in the decision on whether to use a full *Teaching Self-Control* interaction or choose another parenting tool when children lose self-control. In each example, the parents chose methods they thought would work best to teach their kids self-control and other important skills.

As always, we recommend that you continue to use all the CSP teaching interactions to reinforce appropriate behaviors, prevent behavior issues, and address behavior problems when they are small. These interactions also can be helpful when you're teaching your child how to stay calm and maintain self-control.

Effective Praise can be used in situations where children calm down before their behavior gets worse or when they have shown improvement in their ability to calm down on their own. Parents may praise children for trying their own ideas for calming down, for taking time to calm down, for calming down more quickly than in the past, or even for apologizing for things they said or did.

It may sound like this: *"Good job! You remembered to take a deep breath and you calmly said, 'I'm mad' all by yourself.* (Return to original issue.) *Because you did that, we can get back to what's bothering you. Why don't you tell me what's bothering you."*

Preventive Teaching is helpful when parents feel that additional teaching and practicing is needed. Parents can use *Preventive Teaching* to teach a new calming-down strategy or a social skill that may have helped the child in the original situation. *Preventive Teaching* is probably most appropriate when a child's emotional behaviors need attention, but are not overly aggressive or inappropriate.

For example: *"The next time you feel angry, say, 'Mommy, I'm mad.' Then maybe I can help you find a better way to handle it. Let's practice taking deep breaths so that you won't get so upset next time."* (Practice a calming skill.)

Corrective Teaching can also be used after *Follow-Up Teaching.* To be most effective, it's important that a child is calm before starting this interaction.

Corrective Teaching is most appropriate when a child's initial problem behaviors are so disruptive that they must be addressed or when a parent recognizes that a child uses emotional outbursts to avoid consequences. In situations like this, giving a negative consequence becomes necessary to show a child that frequent and severe behaviors only make things worse.

This teaching might sound like this: *"I'm glad you are feeling calmer now. Earlier, you would not stop yelling or go to your room to calm down when I asked. Since you didn't, you will have to sit in Time-Out for five minutes."* (Using Time-Out)

After Time-Out is over, the parent says: *"Thanks for sitting so quietly in Time-Out. Staying calm helps you get more playtime later. Now let's practice what you can do the next time you feel upset."*

(Review the chapters on *Effective Praise, Preventive Teaching,* and *Corrective Teaching* for the specifics of these teaching interactions.)

Summing Up

Responding to a child's emotional outburst is never an enjoyable experience. However, it is an inevitable part of rearing young children. These situations may be few and far between in your family or they may happen more often than you care to admit.

Whether you want to do a little "fine-tuning" in the way you handle these situations or are in need of a fresh start, *Teaching Self-Control* can help. Your calm approach and teaching can help your children make great improvements in this area. Some children catch on quickly, while others may need a little more time. Be patient and look for improvements. Teach your children how to stay calm and give yourself permission to do the same. *Teaching Self-Control* can help with both.

[1] Eisenberg, A., Murkoff, H.E., & Hathaway, S.E. (1994). *What to expect: The toddler years*. New York: Workman Publishing.

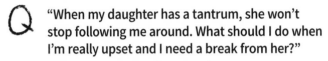

Frequently Asked Questions
about
Teaching Self-Control

Q **"When my daughter has a tantrum, she won't stop following me around. What should I do when I'm really upset and I need a break from her?"**

A At a neutral time, make a *Staying Calm Plan* for yourself. Use *Preventive Teaching* to practice what you and she will do in order to stay calm. Let her know that if she goes to her calm-down place, then you will listen to her sooner. Be aware of her early warning signals. When she begins to get upset, remind her of your agreement. If she does not respond appropriately, focus your attention on other things and calmly wait it out. Use consequences if she continues to follow you around. Eventually she will learn that she will not be able to whine or bully you into doing what she wants.

Q **"How can I correct my child for yelling when I know he is just imitating what I do when I'm mad?"**

A Modeling behavior, both positive and negative, is powerful. Setting a good example will go a long way toward helping your children learn how to handle frustrating situations. Kids learn a lot by watching. So take a deep breath or use another calming strategy to help you control your negative reactions. Learning to respond calmly will not happen overnight, but with effort and an effective *Staying Calm*

Plan, you can do it. In the meantime, continue to use *Corrective Teaching* and *Teaching Self-Control* to deal with misbehaviors.

 "My son doesn't throw a tantrum; he just refuses to do what I ask him to do. Is he out of control and what should I do?"

Yes. He is out of control. Anytime children refuse to correct misbehavior, whether they are being aggressive (having a tantrum) or passive (hiding under a bed), they are out of control. It's important to allow your son time to calm down. Make frequent checks on his ability to cooperate. When he is calm, teach him an acceptable way to express his feelings and give him different, appropriate words to say when he is mad.

 "What if my daughter has a tantrum in the morning when I have to go to work?"

 If this is a frequent problem, you may want to deal with it right there and then. Place her in a safe place, use brief calm-down instructions, and use Time-Out as a consequence. Then continue your morning routine. Don't interact with your child until she is calm. If you have to drive to a day care center or a baby sitter, her Time-Out can take place in her car seat on the way. Set the timer and remind her why she is in Time-Out. While continuing your morning routine, have her practice how to calm down. Remember to use *Preventive Teaching* and *Corrective Teaching* in order to reduce the frequency of these tantrums.

"When my 2-year-old son gets angry, he hits me. What can I do?"

 Hitting is not okay, even if it's a 2-year-old doing it. Firmly say to him, "Hitting hurts people. Don't hit." Then, put him in a safe place and take a break. When things are calmer, teach him what to do instead of hitting. Look at what is frustrating your son and be aware of early warning signals that tell you he is about to hit you. Don't hit him back to show that it hurts; this only models the kind of behavior you're trying to stop.

14

All Together Now!

Enhancing Family Life

· ·

We've talked a lot in this book about the ups and downs of family life, and about what we as parents can do to help our children learn how to behave better. Hopefully, the lessons of *Common Sense Parenting* will be useful as you teach your children the lessons they must learn as they grow up.

From our years of experience working with parents around the world, we know they also want to know about other aspects of parenting that are important in helping shape children's lives. Things like creating family traditions, celebrating holidays and special events, establishing daily routines, and emphasizing family values can enhance life in the home for everyone.

Creating Family Traditions

Traditions are an important part of family life. They help define our families and give them unique identities.

Traditions are the rules, routines, celebrations, and habits that make each family special.

Whether it's a special food or a one-of-a-kind way to observe a holiday, we all know families who do a wonderful job of celebrating themselves with the traditions they have.

Some kids' toys used to be tools. Philippine hunters once used large yo-yos to catch wild animals. In China, kites were flown in patterns to communicate between army camps.

Traditions also create childhood memories and bring family members closer together. Older traditions help link one generation to another as they are passed down from grandparents to parents to children. They give family members a sense of their history. Families also can start new traditions that are then continued as children grow up.

Family traditions can take on many different forms. For most of us, memories of holidays come to mind when we think of family traditions. However, family traditions include other types of family celebrations and activities as well. Family traditions include everything that makes each family special. In this chapter, we will look at four types of family traditions: holidays, special events, daily routines, and family values.

Celebrating Holidays and Special Events

Holiday celebrations are the most common type of family tradition. Families celebrate holidays in many ways. Many have a special meal with extended family or friends. Holiday traditions also may include attending worship services together, giving gifts, or going on an outing together.

Birthdays, weddings, and anniversaries are just some of the special events families celebrate with traditions. Many families also build celebrations around other special events like children's lifetime milestones such as learning to walk, the first day of school, getting a driver's license, and graduating from high school, and major family events like having a child, buying a home, or going on the annual family vacation.

As your family marks holidays or special events, be sure to talk to your children about the specifics of your family celebration, such as who will be attending a family meal or the foods you'll serve. Make sure your children help with planning the celebration and making preparations, such as helping set the table or greeting guests. Your goals should be to make them feel like a valuable part of your family.

Also discuss with your children why the celebration is important. For example, you might explain your family's

Christmas celebration this way to a very young child: *"Our family gets together every year on Christmas. It's a special day, so we want to be together."*

As children grow older, you can provide more details about how your family traditions got started and why they're important. These details will help children understand the traditions so they can carry them on when they are adults or adapt them to their own lives as they get older. Traditions provide each generation with links to the past.

For some people, memories of holidays and special events may not be pleasant. If that is true in your family, try to establish some new traditions with your children to celebrate special times and give new meaning to these special days.

Changes in family life may require changes in family traditions. The death of a family member, divorce, remarriage, or moving to a new home might mean your family has to create new traditions or find a different way to celebrate old traditions.

For example, one family we know moved to a city that was far away from their relatives. Because the family couldn't always travel to be with their relatives on holidays, they began a new tradition of inviting friends and co-workers to share a holiday meal with them.

How families celebrate and honor these types of events can provide many lasting memories, make individuals feel special, and bring extended family together.

Think back to your childhood; what are some special events you remember?

Here are some examples of traditions for celebrating religious or cultural holidays:

* Attend worship services as a family.

* Have a potluck meal for extended family and friends.

* Make special foods that celebrate your family's religious, ethnic, or cultural heritage.

* Have special at-home holiday activities that all family members participate in: decorating your home, preparing food, eating together, watching a favorite family movie or holiday television show, playing games together, taking family pictures.

* Schedule family outings; they can be as elaborate as a winter ski trip or as simple as a walk in the park, a trip to a museum, or jumping in the car and touring the city to look at holiday light displays. Some ideas: Easter egg hunts, holiday caroling, Fourth of July concerts or picnics, holiday shopping trips.

* Spend part of your holiday volunteering as a family at a local soup kitchen or homeless shelter or do some other community service project.

* Talk to your children about their ethnic, cultural, or religious heritage during holidays like Cinco de Mayo, Kwanzaa, St. Patrick's Day, Easter, Christmas,

Hanukkah, First Communion, Confirmation, Bar Mitzvah, or other holidays or religious celebrations.

Here are some ways to celebrate special events in the lives of family members:

Birthdays: The person celebrating the birthday gets to choose the dinner menu. Look at photos from last year's birthday celebration.

Anniversaries: On your anniversary, go through your wedding album, show your kids pictures from your special day, and share memories of what it was like.

Special Accomplishments or Achievements: Celebrate your child's toilet training, the first day of kindergarten, a great day at gymnastics class, being chosen flower girl or ring bearer in a family wedding, and other achievements by taking photos, serving a special meal, going out for dinner, or just talking about the accomplishment and offering praise.

Other Occasions: Getting a new pet might prompt a family gathering to name the animal. You might celebrate moving into a new house or apartment by having a picnic on the floor on moving day.

Following Daily Routines

Believe it or not, everyday routines can also be considered family traditions. There are numerous daily routines that make families special and create lasting memories.

Daily routines can include eating meals together, reading bedtime stories, having a "special" Saturday morning breakfast, prayers at mealtime or bedtime, renting a family movie, and kissing the children as they leave for day care or school.

Other routines may include having children eat all their vegetables, take off their shoes when they enter the house, do homework before watching television, wash their hands before dinner, and help with chores around the house.

Any regular routine that gives a family identity or helps it to get through each day can be considered a family tradition. These routines offer security in that they let family members know when things are normal. Family members feel as though something is missing when one of these habits or routines is not done. These types of routines give children a sense of comfort and safety and can help to build positive habits. Think of some of the daily routines you had as a child; you may want to use some of these with your children or start new daily traditions.

Here are some examples of traditions that can be part of everyday routines:

Morning: Tell everyone *"I love you"* before you leave home. Have breakfast together. If you must leave home before the rest of your family eats breakfast, leave a little *"Have a great day!"* note on the kitchen table.

Evening: Have dinner together, spend time talking about how the day went, read bedtime stories to children, watch a video together, or spend time reading quietly together.

Mealtime: Say grace, have a certain seating arrangement around the table, serve a special food on a certain night (Friday night is pizza night), occasionally let kids choose what's for dinner.

Weekends: Have special Saturday morning or Sunday morning breakfasts or brunches, let children accompany you on errands, have a game night, take a hike or ride bikes together on weekend afternoons, go on a family outing, or go to the library to check out books.

Instilling Family Values

We've described family traditions as celebrations or routines that make families unique, bring members together, and are sometimes passed along from one generation to another.

Family values can be another type of tradition. Family values are those beliefs and habits that family members consider important. They remind family members of what is expected and what one's family stands for. They give us direction and help us make decisions. Family values are the ideals that parents wish to pass on to their children.

Examples of family values include honesty, integrity, citizenship, kindness, patience, forgiveness, self-control, etc. Families live out their values by doing things like sharing, helping others, attending church, planning and saving for the future, spending time together, apologizing for mistakes, showing concern for others, doing one's best, etc.

These values are taught to children (as they listen to what parents say) and are caught by children (as they watch what parents do). Thinking back to your childhood, what are some values your parents demonstrated for you or tried to instill in you?

Summing Up

Think of traditions and daily routines as a way to give three cheers for your family. The activities you choose don't have to be elaborate. The important thing is that you do them and come together as a family.

We think a good way to help you remember the importance of uncomplicated celebrations is to relate the story a friend told us about one of her strongest childhood memories – the summer day decades ago when her mother packed up some peanut butter sandwiches and lemonade and took her two young children into the backyard for an impromptu picnic.

Our friend still remembers what it was like to sit on the ground and feel the grass prickly beneath a bedspread, eat her sandwich, and feel the hot sun on her face.

That mother had a knack for making the simple remarkable. We think that's the whole idea around creating traditions – the ability to create wonderful memories and celebrate without getting lost in the celebration.

It's Just Routine!

Toilet Training, Trips, Bedtime, and Meals

- -

Toilet training, how to behave on outings, and following mealtime and bedtime routines are just a few of the essential skills parents want their children to learn but toddlers may have difficulty with. In this chapter, we'll provide some information and useful ideas on helping young children develop these skills.

Toilet Training

The idea behind the old saying, *"You can lead a horse to water but you can't make him drink,"* is probably the best way to look at training your children to use the toilet. Toilet training is exactly what it says – training. You can provide the training, but ultimately your child will decide when he or she is ready to begin using the toilet.

Before you begin a training program, you need to determine if your child is ready to learn to use the toilet by himself or herself.

Talk to your child's pediatrician for advice on when and how to begin toilet training, and keep the following questions in mind to help you determine if your child has the physical maturity and mental ability to start the process:

* Does my child have an awareness of how his or her body works?

* Does he or she understand what going to the toilet means?

* Does he or she know how to undress and dress?

* Does my child have the physical ability to control bladder and bowels?

* Can my child follow instructions and speak clearly?

Make a big production out of placing your child's potty seat in the bathroom. Show your son or daughter how to use it, and talk about how neat it is. Once you are ready to begin toilet training, try to make the process free of fear and pressure.

When you begin training, let your child use the potty seat as often or as little as he or she wants. You also can use a chart with stickers (see the example on page 134) or some other system to measure your child's attempts, improvements, and accomplishments.

Remember that each child will learn this lesson in his or her own time. Some children can be toilet-trained easily, while other children need lots of time, practice, and supervision. Whatever methods you decide to use, make sure to take your time and use lots of patience. Be sure to praise your children's attempts and reward any improvements. Parents and older siblings also can act as guides by planting seeds of encouragement and talking about how this special event works.

Your main responsibility in the training is to provide your children with the proper tools, such as a safe potty chair that's easy for them to use, and underpants that are easy to pull off and put on.

Also, it's a good idea to think of things that would encourage your children to use the toilet consistently, such as reading special books, having special toys that are used only at potty time, or talking about toilet training advantages. These advantages include being able to spend more time away from home without worrying about diapers.

Nighttime training tips.

Parents often wonder how they should go about teaching their children to wake up during the night to go to the bathroom to prevent bed-wetting. Some parents concentrate on daytime toilet training first and then work on the nighttime training.

Parents might start the nighttime training by using *Preventive Teaching* and practice by waking their children during daytime naps. From there, the next step may be for the parents to wake the child at a certain time each night to use the bathroom. Remember, lots of patience and praise is important. If bed-wetting problems persist after age 6, parents should ask their child's pediatrician for advice.

> "It goes without saying that you should never have more children than you have car windows."
>
> – *Erma Bombeck*

Praise success.

Once your child has accomplished toilet training, be sure to celebrate! You and your child deserve it. You can call grandparents and tell them about your children's success. If a parent has been at work or away during a successful day of training, have your child tell the good news in great detail when the parent gets home. Or make a ceremony out of putting away the diapers and picking out the new cartoon or action figure training pants.

Expect accidents.

When accidents occur, don't make a fuss with negative comments. Simply tell your child how he or she can undo or redo the situation and then offer praise for the effort. It is a mistake to let toilet training become some terrible thing that parents dread and children want to avoid. Instead, make it a special event, with all of its ups and downs, that becomes an important goal your family accomplishes together.

On the Road

With a little teaching, planning, and creativity, you can take your young children on shopping trips or other outings and not have to worry about behavior problems.

First, talk to your children about the trip before you head out the door. Even if you're just going to the grocery store for a few items, tell your children, in simple terms, what you're going to do at the store and how you expect them to behave.

For example, say, *"Myesha, we're stopping at the mall for a minute to pick up Grandma's birthday present. We won't have time to stop at any other stores, so please don't ask to do that. Next time, we'll spend more time at the mall."*

Another way to make a shopping trip easier is to make a game out of it. You could call it a "Store Drill." The game works this way: Bring a small kitchen timer with you in the car. Set it for a reasonable amount of time, based on what you have to do at the store. Tell your children in advance that their role in the game is to go into the store with you as quickly and as quietly as possible without asking you to buy them something or touching anything.

The game gets interesting as you try to beat the clock and your kids try to keep their behaviors appropriate. If you and your kids get back to the car before the timer goes off, and everyone has behaved well, you can offer a special treat.

You can use a similar type of game to encourage good behavior on long car trips. Prepare your children for a long trip by reinforcing good behavior on several smaller trips. Use the techniques of *Preventive Teaching* to teach your children what behaviors you want them to do.

You and your children will feel more confident and comfortable about taking trips when all of you practice ways to better enjoy them.

Some other tips for making trips with young children more enjoyable:

Watch for signs of fatigue.

When children are tired, their ability to follow instructions and behave appropriately declines. Take a break or head home when you know your children are tired or when you're feeling beat.

Bring the right supplies.

Whether it's diapers, toys, books, children's "sippy" cups, or an afternoon snack, make sure you bring along whatever supplies you'll need to sustain young ones for a short or long road trip.

Make children partners in the trip.

Your young children are your traveling companions for the trip, even if it's a quick run for a jug of milk. Talk to them in the car and discuss items you see in the store. Ask them questions. Listen to what they have to say, just as you would with an adult traveling companion. Point out interesting things along the way. Make the trip an opportunity to spend some fun time together.

Bedtime Routines

Bedtime can be a struggle for some families. Some children have difficulty going straight to bed, while others may have problems staying in bed once they have said goodnight. Establishing a bedtime routine is a gentle way for parents to guide children through what can be a difficult time of day.

First, determine what tasks need to be part of that routine, such as taking a bath, brushing teeth, or reading a goodnight story. Then determine how long it will take to complete those tasks. Next, establish a schedule for getting those tasks done each night in time to meet your child's bedtime. Some families schedule these tasks one after the other and right before the child gets into bed. Other families have the tasks scattered throughout the evening.

If you haven't used a schedule, talk to your kids about how it will work and answer any questions they have. Let them know that this is the schedule everyone will be following and then make sure you see that everyone follows it.

Don't be surprised if your kids test the limits at first by stalling to stay up later, arguing, or just not following the schedule. Stay calm and help your children focus on what they should be doing to remain on schedule. For instance, you could simply redirect your child with the statement, *"We are not going to talk about that now. Come with me. Let's get your teeth brushed."*

One way to boost bedtime success is to give your children only one or two instructions at a time instead of rattling off a long list of things for them to do for bedtime.

Another good idea to help keep bedtime blues away is to stay on track once the routine begins. Avoid phone calls and other distractions that get you and your children off task. There may be times when interruptions are unavoidable, but try as much as possible to keep everyone moving toward the same goal.

However you set up the schedule, remember that children respond more enthusiastically to routines when parents participate and offer encouragement, when children have a say in some of the activities, and when the routine is mostly enjoyable.

Some families use a relay-type game to get their bedtime schedule rolling. Children will see the relay as a fun game involving the whole family, and parents will complete important steps to get children ready for bed.

Here's how it works: Right after dessert, create a toothbrush relay. Each member of the family must brush his or her teeth for two minutes. Set a timer so you'll know when the two minutes is up. One person starts, and once the timer goes off, the first person tags a brother, sister, or parent to keep the relay going until everyone has brushed his or her teeth. Whoever is last starts another relay involving putting on pajamas, turning down a bed, kissing everyone goodnight, or other tasks. When the relays end, everyone is

"Babies are necessary to grown-ups. A new baby is like the beginning of all things – wonder, hope, a dream of possibilities. In a world that is cutting down its trees to build highways, losing its earth to concrete… babies are almost the only remaining link with nature, with the natural world of living things from which we spring."

— *Eda J. Le Shan*

ready for bed. Children like the game because it seems like play, and it helps get the routine established.

Other suggestions for having a successful bedtime schedule:

* Follow the same routine every evening, even if your family is traveling.

* Avoid horseplay or roughhousing with young children prior to their getting ready for bed.

* Lower the lights and turn off the television to signal that the evening is winding down. Play soft, relaxing music.

* Read storybooks as a part of the bedtime routine. Make the story an incentive for getting ready for bed. Say, *"If you get your pajamas on and your teeth brushed quickly, we'll have time for a story."*

* Say a bedtime prayer together.

Keeping kids in bed.

So far, we have discussed ways of getting children to go to bed. Now let's review some ideas for keeping them there.

When children have gotten into the habit of getting out of bed frequently, and parents haven't corrected it right away, it may not be easy to change that behavior all at once. Setting boundaries that require your children to stay in bed is the first step toward change. Parents also can create a routine that slowly gets children to go back to bed on their own.

One way to do this is by helping your child create a "stoplight" out of construction paper. Cut out a rectangular piece of paper to serve as the stoplight box, then cut out three green circles and one red circle for the lights. Put masking tape on the back of the green lights so they can easily be attached and removed from the stoplight box. The red light can be taped to the box so it stays attached.

Tell your children that once they have gone to bed, they are allowed to get up only three times for things like a drink of water, an extra kiss good night, or using the toilet. Each time they get up, they must bring you one of the green lights off their stoplight. Parents should say as little as possible and quickly return the child to his or her bedroom after a green light is used.

When children run out of green lights, they are not allowed to get up anymore. The remaining red light on the stoplight tells them they must remain in bed. At this point, parents can say, *"Your red light is on. That means you must stay in bed."* (Of course, if children become scared or are ill, comfort them and don't use the stoplight game.)

As children get better at the game, you can limit them to two green lights, or just one. Be sure to encourage them along the way and celebrate when they start staying in bed.

Parents can also provide some items – a small bedtime book, a favorite stuffed animal, a wind-up tick-tock clock, a special soft blanket, or other safe objects – that children can use to put themselves back to sleep. Another simple method is to tell children they must lie in bed but don't necessarily have to go to sleep. That gives kids the choice of when to sleep and creates a boundary for where and how they sleep on their own.

Dealing with nighttime fears.

Some children's sleep is interrupted by sleepwalking, talking, night terrors, and nightmares. Parents of children who experience these problems should make a point of eliminating vigorous activity and excitement at bedtime.

> Boys are more likely to sleepwalk than girls, and the habit tends to run in families.

Parents also should not give their children foods or drinks that are sugary or have caffeine before bedtime.

For these children, it is very important to establish a regular routine; using safety locks, gates, and practicing relaxation techniques also may be helpful. Don't allow your child to watch aggressive or action-packed television shows before bedtime. Soft music or books can be great tools to slow down children's active imaginations.

Parents should be aware that it is not unusual for young children to experience these sleep interruptions and that they will probably outgrow them in time. Stay calm and comfort your children by allowing them to share their feelings and fears when they are fully awake. If the interruptions increase or grow worse, you may want to consult your pediatrician.

Mealtime Routines

Mealtime can be stressful for families. Young children's changing eating habits and rapid growth frequently cause changes in food preferences. At the same time, many young children are learning that they can make decisions on their own, and they have learned that mealtimes provide opportunities to exercise their independence and explore their limits. Therefore, it's important to establish mealtime rules and routines that help everyone in the family enjoy coming together and sharing a nourishing, healthy meal.

Mealtime routines might include serving meals at about the same time every day, encouraging good manners, eating foods from all the food groups, and trying new foods. Routines also can include having each family member do specific tasks to get the meal on the table and to clean up after the meal is over.

One way to encourage mealtime manners for young children is to use your fingers to keep track of how often a child uses good manners. For example, if a child politely asks for something to be passed to him, that would count as one point (hold up one finger). If the child gets ten points during a meal (one finger for each good manner), he or she might earn the privilege of watching a video or having a special dessert. When young children focus on playing this good manners game, they may become more cooperative at the table.

Another fun way to create a mealtime routine is to let your children be kitchen helpers. Whether it is helping set the table, picking the vegetable they like, stirring their favorite food, cleaning up after the meal with a parent, or just being the one who calls everyone to the meal, this can help children grow to understand they are an important part of the mealtime routine.

Use lots of praise at mealtime and try to avoid argument cycles by planning and practicing ahead of time what will routinely happen when children do or don't participate in mealtime routines.

Emphasize healthy eating at all meals, and serve children healthy snacks such as fruits or vegetables between meals.

Sources for Toilet Training, Trips, Bedtime and Meals

Friman, P.C. (2005). *Good night, sweet dreams, I love you. Now get into bed and go to sleep!* Boys Town: Boys Town Press.

Reimers, T.M. (2011). *Help! There's a toddler in the house! Proven strategies for parents of 2- to 6-year-olds to survive and thrive through the mischief, mayhem, and meltdowns.* Boys Town: Boys Town Press.

16

Putting It All Together

Your Own Parenting Plan

• •

This book is more than a collection of individual chapters on raising young children. All of the skills you have learned in this book are meant to work together. Though they're fine parenting tools by themselves, these skills work much more effectively when they are part of a parenting approach that uses all of them.

For example, *Effective Praise* is a wonderful tool for encouraging your children to do more of the things you like. However, it is not a skill for responding to problem behaviors. *Corrective Teaching* works much better for this purpose. These two skills need to work together to clearly teach children the behaviors they should and shouldn't do and to praise children for steps they make in the right direction.

253

The purpose of this chapter is to clearly show how you can use everything you have learned in this book to develop a parenting style that will allow you to positively and effectively discipline and care for your children. We'll call this your *Common Sense Parenting* Plan. Before we look more closely at creating this plan, there is something important we need to keep in mind.

Beginning with *Effective Praise* and continuing through *Teaching Self-Control*, you have learned parenting skills that empower you to handle most of the day-to-day child discipline issues parents face. However, these skills are just tools for discipline. The real foundation of parenting comprises other things: unconditional love, understanding child development, and nurturing relationships with our children. Let's look at these briefly.

Unconditional love.

Unconditional love for our children is the cornerstone of parenting. It provides an environment in which nurturing and learning can occur. Children need to feel safe to try new things, even if it means occasional failure. They need to know they are loved and valued because of who they are, not what they do. Children need to feel they belong and are accepted even though they are not perfect. Unconditional love from parents sends children these messages. Discipline works best when it is administered by a loving adult in a positive, teaching way.

Understanding child development.

Understanding how our children grow and learn helps us know what we can reasonably expect of them and when they are ready for our teaching. The skills in this book are more likely to be effective when they are used in ways that are appropriate for your child's physical and emotional development. Remember that the keys to teaching young children include repetition, consistency, and patience.

Nurturing relationships.

Nurturing children may be the greatest use of a parent's time. Besides loving their children unconditionally, there is no other more important responsibility parents have than helping them grow up happy, healthy, and confident. Chores and household tasks will be around for us to do whether we do them now or later. Issues such as toilet training, children's messy bedrooms, and bath time hassles will come and go. Eventually, children grow out of diapers, learn to feed and dress themselves, and take care of many of their own needs. Some problems may linger for a while, but even those tend to go away as our children turn into young adults and venture out on their own. Nurturing them is the way we prepare them for that time.

The only part of parenting that truly lasts is our relationship with our children. It begins prior to birth and continues long after our children are grown and gone.

Strong relationships help us cherish the good times and get through the tough times. However, relationships don't just happen.

Strong relationships are built on shared experiences and commitment. They require time. There is no such thing as unimportant time with a child. Every bedtime story, every kiss on the cheek, and every trip to the park helps to nurture a parent-child relationship.

Relationships also are nurtured in how you discipline your children. This occurs when you praise often, teach your children how to be successful, set appropriate limits for them, and stay calm when your child is not. How you discipline your children can show them how much you care for them.

Each day, we are all given the same amount of time to spend. Use your time well and spend as much of it as possible on the things that have lasting significance, especially your relationship with your child.

Common Sense Parenting Plan

Now that we have the foundation in place, let's move on to creating a plan for effectively teaching our children.

Step 1: Identify the problem.

Although a parenting plan may begin with teaching new skills and routines or strengthening existing ones, such plans usually are developed because of a child's problem behavior.

Before a change can take place, parents need to first clearly identify the problem. That means developing a clear description of what a child is doing or saying and what the parent wishes to change. To begin making a *Common Sense Parenting Plan* of your own, think of one child behavior problem you would like to change and write that problem down on a sheet of paper entitled *"My Common Sense Parenting Plan."* (A sample *Common Sense Parenting Plan* is included at the end of this chapter to give you some ideas on how to complete your plan.)

> "When you help a child today, you write the history of tomorrow."
>
> – *Father Flanagan*

Step 2: Teach alternatives.

The second step of your plan is to identify how you would like your child to behave differently. Usually, specific teaching or making a change in a routine can help things go better. The teaching may focus on a specific task or social skill you would like your child to do.

Think of one or two things you could teach that would help your child to be more successful in the problem situation you identified. On your *Common Sense Parenting*

Plan sheet, write down how you could teach this to your child using *Preventive Teaching*.

Step 3: Encourage positive changes.

Once you begin proactively teaching your child how to be more successful, the next step is to keep encouraging changes to continue. This can be done by using *Effective Praise* when a child shows improvements or tries to do better.

Remember, making changes can be difficult for children. You may also need to use occasional rewards (positive consequences) to encourage your child to keep trying to do better or to maintain changes that have already occurred. On your *Common Sense Parenting Plan* sheet, write down how you could use *Effective Praise* and rewards to encourage positive changes in your child's behavior.

> "Children need love, especially when they don't deserve it."
>
> – *Harold Hulbert*

Step 4: Correct mistakes.

No matter how well we teach and encourage our children to do better, they will probably still make some mistakes before things start to get better. When this happens, you can use *Corrective Teaching* and a negative consequence to stop the problem behavior and teach your children how to do better the next time.

On your sheet, write down how you could use *Corrective Teaching* if your child continues to do the problem behavior and what negative consequences may be effective in helping him or her focus on positive behaviors.

Step 5: Plan to stay calm.

With some behaviors, things may seem to get worse before they get better. Young children can easily become angry, embarrassed, or frustrated when they are corrected or when they are trying to learn something new. Parents can also feel frustrated or angry when changes are slow to occur.

To help ensure that your emotions do not get in the way of your teaching, you may need to combine your *Staying Calm Plan* with the skill of *Teaching Self-Control*. On your sheet, write down how you and your child can calm down if emotions run high as you work with your child on the problem behavior you've identified.

Helpful Hints

That's it! You have now created a sound plan for changing a problem situation with your child. Let this be your guide to help you calmly and purposefully teach your child to make positive changes in this problem area.

Use a plan like this for other child behavior problems. To make your plan more effective, remember the following helpful hints:

Be consistent.

Young children learn best through repetition and consistency. Effective parenting is not rocket science. Rather, it is a few simple things done consistently. Use the *Common Sense Parenting* skills you've learned to help you consistently teach your children the lessons they need to learn.

Focus on the positive.

Lessons that grow in the fertile soil of encouragement will last longer than those that struggle on the rocky ground of criticism. Look for your child's improvements and attempts to do well. Correcting problem behaviors will always be part of parenting. Praise and encouragement become an effective part of parenting only if you intentionally include them.

Be creative.

Rearing young children should be fun and exciting. Look for opportunities to make everyday events special and reinforcing for you and for your child. Practice with games and make-believe, look at things from your child's point of view, and let your child teach something to you.

Other creative ways to teach include putting expectations to song, using humor, and using charts or stickers to keep track of successes. These types of ideas may also help reduce stress, increase motivation, and strengthen your relationship with your child. When problems persist, don't be afraid to try a new approach or to reach out to others for help. Talk to day care and preschool staff, read other books on parenting, watch other parents, call friends and relatives, or visit Boys Town's **parenting.org** website.

Reward yourself.

Some of the biggest struggles in rearing young children involve feelings of being overworked, underappreciated, and alone. Rearing young children is a big responsibility. Sometimes the work it requires makes it difficult to see the joys and benefits. Young children don't understand what it means to have a long day at work, to worry about bills, or to have housework piling up. They just want to play. It is easy for parents to make their own tasks the focus of day-to-day life. Then, before they know it, they realize they haven't done anything for themselves in a long, long time.

Just like an automobile, you cannot run on empty for very long. What refills your tank? Take a few minutes to think about what may help you feel energized, hopeful, or appreciated. Here are a few ideas:

* Enjoying a long bubble bath
* Having a date night with spouse

* Attending an adult church service with no children
* Seeing a movie with friends
* Buying a new outfit
* Dining out (with no children)
* Going to a ballgame
* Going to a play or a movie
* Using paper plates so you don't have to wash dishes
* Spending time on a hobby or sport
* Working out
* Sleeping in
* Getting dressed with no kids under foot
* Going on a walk
* Listening to your favorite music
* Having time to read
* Taking turns baby-sitting with other parents
* Using "Mother's Day Out" services provided by some churches
* Having relatives or friends baby-sit your children regularly
* Playing golf or cards with friends

Select a few items from this list or create your own list. You may choose to do some activities with your entire family or enjoy others by yourself or with other adults. Make a plan to include some of these in your schedule.

Use these ideas to reward yourself for following your *Common Sense Parenting* Plan or just because you need an occasional break. However you decide to fit these into your schedule, one thing is a must – fit them in. All parents need encouragement, something to look forward to, and ways to reduce the stress of everyday life. Identify ways to meet these needs and make them a regular part of your life. Both you and your children will benefit.

Summing Up

We hope that as you use the skills from this book, you will begin to see positive changes in your children and in yourself. Will you see all of the stress and problems of parenting disappear? Will you have the perfect answer for every issue that arises? Of course not. No parenting program can make such promises.

However, we are confident that the skills you have learned can help you with most of the day-to-day issues you face. Why are we so confident? For two reasons. First, we have seen these skills work well with families just like yours. Parents who use the skills taught in *Common Sense Parenting* report fewer child behavior problems, and they tell us they feel more satisfied with their family and in their role as parents.

The other reason for our confidence is **YOU!** Parents of young children are among the most amazing people we meet. Parents of toddlers and preschoolers regularly exhibit some of the greatest parenting qualities, including love, commitment, care and concern, patience, ability to listen, willingness to sacrifice, humor, creativity, flexibility, excitement over child successes, ability to forgive mistakes, and willingness to learn.

It's true that the parenting skills presented in this book are effective in rearing young children. However, these skills are of little use without you and your commitment to your children. The qualities you bring to parenting are what truly make a difference in the life of your child. This is true while your children are young, and it is also true as your children grow into young adults.

Celebrate your children's successes and the milestones they reach. You are a big reason for each accomplishment. Don't let setbacks or struggles get you down. Remember, as you stay involved in your child's life, you have the opportunity to help turn setbacks into future successes. Continue to enjoy your children and allow them to enjoy you.

Sample Common Sense Parenting Plan

Step 1: Identify the problem.

A behavior my child does that I would like to change:

He leaves his toys all over the living room.

Step 2: Teach alternatives.

One thing I could change that would help with the problem is:

Not allow toys in the living room, only in the bedroom or playroom.

Two things I could teach my child that would help with the problem are:

Following instructions to pick up toys when he is asked.

Asking permission to get toys out before he brings them to the living room.

Step 3: Encourage positive changes.

Improvements or positive attempts I could praise my child for are:

Saying "Okay" when he is asked to pick up toys.

Staying calm when he is asked to pick up toys.

Picking up some of his toys.

Accepting a negative consequence when he leaves his toys out.

Rewards I can use are:

Praise, smiles, touches, helping pick up toys, cookie, playing together.

Step 4: Correct mistakes.

What I could say when correcting my child for leaving his toys out:

Show and Tell the problem behavior: *"Honey, I know you want to watch television, but your toys are still on the floor."*

Give a negative consequence: *"You won't be able to watch television until your toys are put away."*

Show and Tell the desired behavior: *"Put all of your toys in the toy box in your bedroom and tell me when you are done."*

Give a reason: *"When you put your toys away, they won't get stepped on."*

Practice: *"Let's see how fast you can do that. I'll time you. Ready? On your mark... Get set... Go!"*

Negative consequences I can use when my child leaves toys out are:

Undo – picking up the toys.

Time-Out.

Redirect him from what he is doing to go back and pick up toys.

Take away the privilege of watching television until toys are picked up.

Step 5: Plan to stay calm.

If I become upset when my child leaves his toys out, I can calm down by:

Taking a deep breath, counting to ten, giving myself a Time-Out.

If my child becomes upset when I talk to him about leaving his toys out, he may be able to calm down by:

Having time alone in his room, taking a deep breath, squeezing his pillow.

Bibliography

Berk, L.F. (1996, 2012). *Infants, children, and adolescents.* Boston: Allyn & Bacon.

Developmental Milestones. (2014, March 27). Centers for Disease Control and Prevention. Retrieved July 31, 2014, from http://www.cdc.gov/NCBDDD/actearly/milestones/index.html

Eisenberg, A., Murkoff, H.E., & Hathaway, S.E. (1994). *What to expect: The toddler years.* New York: Workman Publishing.

Franck, I., & Brownstone, D. (1996). *Parenting A to Z.* New York: Harper Collins.

Friman, P.C. (2005). *Good night, sweet dreams, I love you. Now get into bed and go to sleep!* Boys Town: Boys Town Press.

Manczak, D.W. (1986-1997). *Normal childhood development.* Greenwood Village, CO: National Health Enhancement Systems, Clinical Reference Systems, Ltd.

Reimers, T.M. (2011). *Help! There's a toddler in the house! Proven strategies for parents of 2- to 6-year-olds to survive and thrive through the mischief, mayhem, and meltdowns.* Boys Town: Boys Town Press.

Shelov, S.P., & Hannemann, R.E. (1993, 2009). *Caring for your baby and young child: Birth to age 5.* New York: Bantam Books.

Thompson, C.E. (1992). 101 *Wacky facts about kids.* New York: Scholastic, Inc., Parachute Press.

White, B.L. (1995). *The first three years of life.* New York: Simon and Schuster.

Index

Q

R